THE FREE MARKET PROGRESSIVE MANIFESTO

APRIL 26, 2017 DRAFT FOR COMMENT

HE

REE

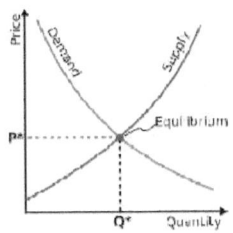

ARKET

R GRE$$IVE

ANIFE$T

R.W. KROEKER

© 2017 Randall W. Kroeker

ISBN: 978-1-365-17381-3

Contact author and self-publisher at:
randy.kroeker@gmail.com
613-716-7272

INTRODUCTION

The purpose of this work is to outline my perception of the limitations of modern liberalism, conservatism, and libertarianism, and propose a direction for correcting these limitations. Part of that process is to review the history of political parties and economics to inform how we got to this point.

I assert that while "classical" progressivism most reflects the better angels of human nature, modern progressivism took a wrong turn post-WW II into well-intended but misguided socialistic, anti-market objectives.

Socialism, if we extend it the benefit of the doubt, has its heart in the right place but is proven more effective at enriching unproductive statists, labourists, crony capitalists, and intellectuals, than the poor.

It is the jealous religion of those who cannot fathom the financial alchemy of the unfettered marketplace.

Modern conservatism, on the other hand, is grossly misnamed, seeking to conserve nothing, as it is in reality, a revolutionary call to arms against the establishment cabal of statists, labourists, crony capitalists and intellectuals.

Libertarianism, a fusion of economic conservatism and social liberalism, while useful as an analytical lens regarding the application of economics upon able individuals, is in its purest social Darwin form, a violation of the empathetic impulse of human nature toward the "worthy poor".

While compassionate, a.k.a. bleeding heart conservatism reflects the best hope for an optimal balance between human compassion and economic effectiveness, it sadly bears the baggage of a public perception of conservatism being relatively heartless, a reactionary longing for the past, in contrast to the perception of modern socialistic, or more accurately, Robin Hood (redistributionist) liberalism.

The resolution of the problem is to reclaim progressivism under the banner of Free Market Progressivism, largely based on the thinking and effective compassion of Mont Pellerin Society members such as Ludwig von Mises, F. A. Hayek, Milton Friedman, Charles Koch and others, notwithstanding their self-identification as ideological libertarians.

It is simply compassionate conservatism, intelligently rebranded and then tweaked toward effective compassion, that follows the best that economic science has to offer. The objective is not only to say more directly what it is, but by calling it a manifesto, I am seeking, only partly tongue-in-cheek, to declare an ideological and political call to arms against the destructiveness and lost opportunities of statism.

The tone is meant to be non-academic, informal and fun; targeting persons passionate about politics, but with no formal training in political science, political history, or economics. To a great extent each sub-chapter one-pager stands on its own. They are somewhat arbitrarily grouped into chapters by theme, such as Europe, North America, political parties, and so on.

Chapter 1 is a review of the European context of progressivism, the progressive struggles of the Roundheads, Whigs and classical liberals, the disaster of the Labour Party and the Thatcher course-correction. Chapter 2 covers the reforms of both Roosevelts as well as Kennedy and Johnson, and the Reagan and Clinton course corrections. Chapter 3 covers the origins of American and Canadian political parties.

Chapter 4 is a speculative historical fable to the end of defending work, thrift, savings, capital, investment, entrepreneurship, employment, money, and banking, to the layperson, most importantly identifying wealth as delayed gratification at scale. Chapter 5 outlines the key contributions of Adam Smith, the father of economics, Carl Menger, founder of the Austrian School, Ludvig von Mises, who first raised the alarm regarding socialism, F.A. Hayek, founder of the Mont Pellerin Society, and Joseph Schumpeter, on entrepreneurship.

Chapter 6 presents key living thinkers and communicators of the current era, Hernando De Soto Polar on property rights, Steven Levitt on incentives, Bjorn Lomborg on environmentalism, Irving Kirzner on economic ignorance, and more controversially, Republican nemesis George Soros on market bubbles.

Chapter 7 addresses the issues of savings, capital, the rich, crony capitalism, the Koch Brothers' role in all this, and Arthur Brooks' moral argument for free enterprise. Chapter 8 takes the reader through an intuitive explanation of supply and demand for the layperson. Chapter 9 delves into the many ways government fails and why. Chapter 10 covers communism, socialism, unions, liberalism, poverty, and Milton Friedman's negative income tax solution to poverty.

Chapter 11 covers the varieties of conservatism, neoconservatism, Ayn Rand, and David Frum on why Republicans lose. Paleo and social conservatives are not discussed in this work intentionally, thinking that opening up a second front would be a distraction. Chapter 12 examines libertarianism, compassionate conservatism, and the proposed solution of reframing compassionate conservatism as free market progressivism.

The structure of this document draws on my experience writing one-page briefing notes for government senior management. The intention is for the reader to begin with the subjects that catch their curiosity, check them off, and then proceed to the next topic that draws their attention. The document is evergreen and evolving genetically, with each one-page sub-chapter section raising questions for further investigation and write-up.

CHAPTER 1 – EUROPEAN PROGRESSIVISM

PHILOSOPHICAL GENESIS OF PROGRESSIVISM

"Philosophy, is the talk on the cereal box"
Edie Brickell

Prussian Immanuel Kant (1724-1804), in the 18th Century, first introduced the idea that humanity was "progressing" from barbarism to civilization.

His view was that humanity had evolving capacities that could not be completed in one lifetime, rather it was an ongoing project over many generations.

He asserted that this potential could not be achieved without peace and that peace would only occur under democracy as citizens would never vote to pay for war.

Immanuel Kant, father of progressivism.

German Georg Hegel (1770-1831) subsequently argued that it was a *linear* progression. These two thoughts launched progressivism, as a political philosophy. He disagreed with Kant in part, asserting that war was part of human nature, and included the benefit of pulling societies together to work on a common goal.

Karl Marx (1818–1883) equally valued the role of conflict between emerging productive forces versus vested historical groups. He had an observation and an assertion. Firstly, the productive, urban, free trading Whig and subsequent Conservative Party merchant class won a necessary victory over the rural, agrarian, feudal, protectionist, Tory aristocracy, launching capitalism. Secondly, this would be followed by a conflict between these same merchants and productive workers, which would resolve itself with the emergence of communism.

Where Marx and the economic theory of the era were in error was an under-appreciation of the essential role of invention, entrepreneurship, savings, and capital, in an evolved economy.

French sociologist Auguste Comte (1798–1857) envisioned a socialist society governed by an unelected elite, advised by a priesthood of social scientists, without facing the hard problem of who then, if not the citizens, choose this unelected elite.

John Stuart Mill (1806–1873) opposed Comte's anti-democratism fearing that unelected institutions were more likely to resist progress than promote it. Herbert Spencer (1820–1903) described progress as the evolution of humans from selfishness to selflessness.

BRITISH PROGRESS

While Europe was busy pondering progressivism, Great Britain was getting on with it.

England had a strong tradition of the rule of law and respect for contracts tracing back to the Magna Carta when the lords first began to seize power from the monarch.

It also had a flexible system of legal jurisprudence which permitted judges to interpret the law and create precedence, in contrast to continental civil code which granted the courts little leeway.

Britain Leads the Industrial Revolution

Further, the domestic peace that followed the political and economic unification of England and Scotland in 1707 established an environment conducive to Kantian, peaceful, progress, in contrast to brief periods of fragile peace on the continent.

In addition, Adam Smith's Wealth of Nations (1776) inspired the gradual disassembling of tariffs and mercantile monopolies in favour of free-market capitalism throughout Great Britain.

In contrast, the Prussian Historical (Economic) School of Germany dominated continental thinking. Its focus was the restoration of Prussia's former statist glory, which pointed to and justified big government. In contrast, an Austrian School grew out of Carl Menger's direct observation of markets as a financial journalist in the 19th century. The Austrians effectively picked up where Adam Smith left off, advancing economics as a market-based science. This vein of market-based economics was later embraced by the Chicago School.

Of paramount importance, Britain actually invented the concept of open administrative access to incorporation with *The Joint Stock Companies Act of 1844*. Significantly, this change ended the age of exploitative mercantilist monopolies granted solely by royal or parliamentary charter. The change was further strengthened by *The Limited Liability Act of 1856*, which encouraged entrepreneurs to attempt new ventures without risking personal bankruptcy.

Progress pushed forward with the application of horse, water, and coal-fired steam-powered mills. These were largely applied to newly invented textile machinery in Manchester, the world's first industrialized city, nicknamed at the time "Cottonopolis".

Powered mills plus greater efficiencies in the production of iron and the invention of steel caused the standard of living for the average person to double in the 19th century, a paradigm shift of equal significance to the domestication of animals, plants and fire.

MERCANTILISM

Mercantilism was the dominant economic theory in the west when Adam Smith took pen to paper with *The Wealth of Nations* (1776), in fierce opposition to it. He argued that it was a mass conspiracy of crown-granted monopolies to rip off consumers. This had the unintended consequence of limiting the overall economic progress and power of the nation.

Mercantilist Gold Accumulation

Mercantilism, as a world view, succeeded the medieval scholastic theorists who considered individual economic relations within the context of the Christian teachings of piety and justice. Its contribution to progress was to put all of a nation's resources to work, all land to agriculture or mining, and all citizens to engagement in productive activity.

The principle objective of mercantilism was for the crown to accumulate as much gold and silver as possible by encouraging the export of finished goods in exchange for bullion. To conserve gold they discouraged imports by means of tariffs, especially of finished goods, and most certainly discouraged payment for imports with bullion.

Shipping and colonies were acquired and regulated to feed this objective. There was the belief that higher wages, leisure and education would be unhelpful to workers as they inherently lacked the capacity to benefit from such measures. Adam Smith offered one path to progress beyond this, and Karl Marx offered another.

Mercantilist Economics was considered a zero-sum game, a fixed beggar (impoverish) thy neighbour economic pie, simply to be sliced up through economic warfare with other nations and with the working classes. This view was superseded by David Ricardo's international pro-trade *Theory of Comparative Advantage* and John Locke's *Labour Theory of Value*.

The latter, a favorite of the left, confuses the value of things with the cost of things, a fatal error in that it is the value of things to the consumer which drives an industry or economy toward the opportunities of the future.

The Mercantilist system worked very well for the crown and the likely less than 1% of the population who were crony merchants. The crown accumulated gold bullion to pay off war debts and to finance the next war, as well as to pay for the acquisition and control of colonies. In the decades following the *Wealth of Nations*, Great Britain moved to freer trade as Parliament took power from the crown. Free trade did not come to France until the revolution, and mercantilism persisted in Germany until the early 20th century, under the influence of the statist Historical school of economics.

CAVALIERS AND ROUNDHEADS

In 1066, King William I (1028-1087) established a royal advisory council (a precedent to Parliament) of landowners and church leaders, who by 1215 forced King John (1166-1216) to accept the *Magna Carta*, which barred new taxes without their approval.

By 1642 the short-haired republican "Roundheads", arose in opposition to the long-locked, royalist, establishment, Church of England "Cavaliers".

During this struggle the New Model Army was formed in 1645, dominated by Roundhead Puritans who opposed the Catholic practices of the Church of England. Not all Roundheads were Puritan, but all Puritans were Roundheads. Some Puritans remained within the Church and lobbied for reform; others were separatists of the ilk represented on the Mayflower.

Cromwell Stages Coup and Kills King

The New Model Army, reporting directly to Parliament, was a check on King Charles I's (1600–1649) power, ultimately defeating the royalist Cavaliers in the English Civil War in 1646. Tension subsequently arose when Cavalier Parliamentarians led an effort to reestablish the absolute power of the monarch.

This risked placing the Puritan and Roundhead Army under the control of the king, the Church of England and the Cavaliers. This was not acceptable to the reformers, intellectuals, Puritans, and soldiers who had just defeated the Cavaliers. Consequently, General Oliver Cromwell (1599-1658), a fanatical Puritan, staged the only military coup in British history, the second British Civil War.

In 1649, Cromwell locked the supporters of the king out of Parliament, executed the king and established a republic (no monarch). When the remaining Rump Parliament refused to give up the state monopoly of the Church of England, he dismissed these representatives, replacing them with selected "pious members of society", but this "Assembly of Saints" failed to work together.

Giving up on democracy, Cromwell acquired the role of Lord Protector for life in 1653. He was offered the crown in 1657, which he refused on principle. His much weaker son Richard succeeded him in 1658 but a crisis emerged as he failed to inspire the Army, and Parliament opposed his legitimacy.

Consequently, the Army leadership retreated from republicanism, reorganized Parliament, and Charles I's son, Charles II, was invited to resume the throne. They backdated his reign as though the Republic had never happened. The Anglican Church returned to persecuting the Catholics and Puritans. Theatres and pubs, closed by the Puritans, reopened.

TORIES, WHIGS, CONSERVATIVES, AND
LIBERALS

Charles II (1630-1685) failed to produce an heir,
which left his Catholic brother James II next in
line to the throne. The Country Party of the rural
landed (land holding) gentry, in 1678, was
attempting to block this and establish
Parliament's right to break hereditary succession.
The Tory Party, ideological descendants of the
royalist Cavaliers, arose to oppose this attempt.

The name Tory derived from the Irish insult
"Torai", meaning outlaw, arising during an
episode of suspicion that Irish Catholic royalists
were plotting to support an invasion by
(Catholic) France.

*Peel Founds Conservative
and Liberal Parties*

James II became king regardless, and everyone's worst fears materialized when he
baptized his son Catholic, pushing aside as heir his older Protestant daughter
Princess Mary. The baptism was too much even for the Tories. The situation was
resolved in 1688 when Princess Mary's Dutch husband Prince William III of
Orange (1650-1702), a champion of Protestantism, invaded at the invitation of
Parliament. This coup was called the "Glorious Revolution." William became *joint*
constitutional monarch with his wife Mary, reinforcing the precedent of Parliament-
centred government. The Protestant Orange Order is named after William of
Orange. James II fled to France and supporters of the restoration of his Catholic line
were called Jacobeans, derived from the Latin for James.

In 1715, the Whigs came to power for the first time and purged the Tories from
leadership positions in the army, church, and government. The name "Whig"
derived from the Scottish insult "Whiggamore", which meant cattle driver. They
were the ideological descendants of the republican Roundheads. By 1760, the Tory
party had dissolved and a Tory came to mean merely a Whig who was particularly
friendly with the King. However, the "New Tories" resurrected themselves by the
turn of the century.

Under industrialist Robert Peel's (1788-1850) *Tamworth Manifesto* (1834), they
blended the reform orientation of the industrial class with the traditional orientation
of the landed gentry, moving sharply beyond monarchy-centric "Old Toryism". The
theme was the evolutionary "Reform to Survive", adopting the label
"Conservatives".

The tension between Peel's industrialist, liberal-on-trade Conservatives, and
Benjamin Disraeli's protectionist, landed gentry Conservatives, broke the party
apart over needed grain tariff reductions brought in by Peel to help with the Irish
famine. Disraeli drove Peel from leadership, possibly motivated by bitterness over
being left out of the earlier Peel Cabinet. Peel left the party, taking the free trading
"Liberal-Conservatives" with him. In 1859 the Liberal-Conservative Peelites joined
with the Whigs and Radicals to form the Liberal Party.

BRITISH LABOUR PARTY

In 1832, the Whigs standardized suffrage (voting) rules in England and Wales, extending voting beyond landowners to land renters and rural heads of households.

1867 reforms extended voting to urban working class men who were heads of households. This growing group of working class voters eventually became convinced that the Liberals were not sufficiently motivated to oppose to the Conservatives. The Independent Labour Party, the intellectual Fabian Society and the Marxist Social Democratic Federation grew out of this dissatisfaction.

U.K. Labour Party Nationalizes Key Industries

In 1899, Thomas R. Steels convinced the Trade Union Congress to bring all left-wing organizations under one Labour umbrella for fielding candidates. They initially leaped ahead in 1906 for two reasons. Firstly, there was a strategic campaign to minimize vote splitting in cooperation with the Liberals. Secondly, there was negative public reaction to a legal ruling that firm owners could recoup the cost of strikes from the unions, which the Conservatives had supported.

Suffrage was further extended in 1918 to include all men over the age of 21 as well as propertied women over the age of 30. This extension and the decline of the Liberal Party in the 1920s permitted Labour to move into the second position in Parliament in 1922. In 1924, Labour first formed a government as a minority, but only with the support of the Liberals, who greatly constrained their socialist designs. The coalition collapsed within the year, putting the Conservatives back in power.

Labour was returned to minority government with Liberal support in 1929. However, the depression overwhelmed the political system and a crisis "National Government" was formed of all parties. This coalition held power until 1940 when it was replaced by the "Coalition Government." Non-coalition rumps of the Labour and Liberal Parties continued in opposition throughout the 1930s.

Labour won its first majority in 1945, unseating the bewildered war hero Winston Churchill, launching the socialist experiment. Mining, steel, coal, electricity, gas, railroads, canals, and transport were nationalized and the cradle to grave welfare state was developed, including the National Health Service. India, Pakistan, Burma, and Ceylon were granted independence. The Party was reelected with an unstable minority in 1950 and further "reforms" were stalled due to severe fiscal pressure from the Korean War. Rationing of food and clothing was still in place from WW II.

THE IRON LADY

When the Conservatives returned to power in 1951 they accepted most of the postwar Labour reforms, which became known as the "post-war consensus." It would be 13 years before the British public would be ready for another round of Labour government.

Successive Labour governments were moderate. Runaway inflation in the 1970s, as high as 24%, was addressed by Labour with wage and price controls, which enraged the unions. This rage culminated with the "Winter of Discontent" in 1979. Following a decade of economic crisis, there were a series of widespread strikes that disrupted British life, the last four years under Labour.

Thatcher Reverses Nationalization of Industries

It was on this wave of discontent and alarm with the public sector unions that Margaret Thatcher came to power in 1979. Thatcherism was largely about rolling back much of the post-war consensus. Many industries were privatized and deregulated and social programs were adjusted. The policy counter-reforms included decoupling of taxes from income levels and property values (to reduce disincentives to work), reforming the National Health Service and selling public housing to residents. Most of these reforms followed the views of Milton Friedman, author of "Free to Choose."

Thatcher Quotes:

"Every family should have the right to spend their money, after tax, as they wish, and not as the government dictates. Let us extend choice, extend the will to choose and the chance to choose."

"No one would remember the Good Samaritan if he'd only had good intentions; he had money as well."

"We Conservatives hate unemployment."

"To cure the British disease with socialism was like trying to cure leukemia with leeches."

"One of the great problems of our age is that we are governed by people who care more about feelings than they do about thoughts and ideas."

"Look at a day when you are supremely satisfied at the end. It's not a day when you lounge around doing nothing, it's a day when you've had everything to do, and you've done it."

ORIGIN OF RIGHT AND LEFT WING

In 1789 France was bankrupt by war, colonies and famine. The clergy (First Estate) and nobility (Second Estate) were exempt from taxes and would not agree to reforms. Exasperated, the King convened an Estates-General, the first in 175 years, which included "the common people" (Third Estate).

Outvoted by the clergy and nobles, who blocked reform, the Third Estate consequently broke off with the Estates-General. Initially remaining loyal to the king himself, they met under the label "National Assembly", with many nobles, most non-leadership clergy, and the moneyed business class supporting the movement.

Those Loyal to the King Sat to the Right of His Chair

The ideological composition of the National Assembly was not homogeneous. In the months leading up to the French revolution, there was a shrinking faction in the National Assembly that remained loyal to the monarch as well as the church, comprised of the uncompromising *Legitimists* and the more moderate, constitutional *Orleanists*.

They faced daily verbal abuse from the revolutionary *Jacobin Club* (named after the location of their first meeting and not associated with English Catholic royalist Jacobitism) and the extremist *Montagnard* members.

Over time, they found themselves clumping together in the Assembly for their own protection and mutual support. It is speculated that the impulse to gather to the right of the King's chair likely goes back to the primordial view of those on the "right hand" of an authority figure being in a relationship of trust and loyalty. This goes at least as far back as biblical references to the position of privilege being on the right hand of God, probably stemming from right-handedness being the human norm.

Sitting on the right was adopted as accepted practise with the more radical members sitting on the left by default. Following the French revolution, the habit reconstituted itself with the more rigid constitutionalists sitting on the right and those calling for further reform on the left. The extremity of views was reflected in how far right or left they sat in the Assembly. Moderates sat in the centre, left-leaners sat centre-left, and right-leaners sat centre-right, with Assembly position becoming official party names.

This concept crossed the channel to England. Right wing, stemming from this original "Tory" loyalty to the King and Church of England, became associated with attachment to the status quo, the past, and the established landed gentry and their protective mercantilist grain tariffs.

AMERICAN INDUSTRIALIZATION

Unregulated industrialization contained a self-limiting Achilles heal, which was market concentration, especially in the United States.

Market concentration enabled anti-competitive behaviour, such as buying up and threatening smaller companies, which paved the way for oligopolies (few sellers) and monopolies (one seller).

Rockefeller, King of the Robber Barons

By the late 19th century, several monopolistic holding company "trusts" had established a stranglehold on the American economy, most prominently, J. D. Rockefeller's (1839-1937) Standard Oil and J.P. Morgan's (1837-1913) U.S. Steel. These trusts were a precursor to the modern holding company. They formed to get around laws against companies formally owning other companies at the time.

Interestingly, Rockefeller's father, a small-time grifter, would cheat his children with money "to keep them sharp". Rockefeller himself practised Social Darwinism in business affairs, running hundreds of small entrepreneurs out of business through anti-competitive practices, later made illegal. On the other hand, he is credited with having invented modern philanthropy at scale, after becoming the richest person in history, by some measures.

These anti-competitive practices were an authentic failure of the market, a failure of "laissez-faire". Over time, these trusts were increasingly and accurately perceived to be a barrier to "progress" and became enemies of the progressive movement. There was at the same time increasing violence between industrialists and the workers who were trying to unionize.

Other market failure challenges arose and were addressed, including: commercial exploitation of natural wonders; exploitation and manipulation of workers on the one hand; and abuse of firm owners by unions on the other hand; fraud regarding consumer goods; unequal treatment of companies dependent on the railway trusts; and the inability of private entities to harness dam and irrigation technology for the purpose of opening up arid ground to agriculture.

At the close of the 19th century, President William McKinley (1843-1901) initiated an investigation into the trusts, launching the Republican Progressive Era, which was equally concerned about industry, party and government corruption. He passed the *Sherman Anti-Trust Act*. While it was not effectively enforced during his presidency, it laid the groundwork for what was to come next.

TEDDY'S SQUARE DEAL

At the turn of the century, New York State Republican governor and progressive Teddy Roosevelt (1858-1919) was perceived to be a radical reformer, a threat to the status quo, the political machine, and the trusts.

He was lured into the vice-presidency, partly out of a belief that this would sideline him politically and prevent him from ever achieving the presidency. It was rare for a vice-president move into the oval office.

President McKinley being shot by anarchist Leon Czolgosz in 1901 was not part of the plan. Based on McKinley's and Senator Sherman's earlier work, many trusts were broken by Roosevelt, a

Reformer Teddy Roosevelt Accidentally Becomes President

key progressive victory. It was as well a victory for economics over authentic "market failure", at a time when Adam Smith economics and progressivism were marching arm in arm.

The Square Deal and subsequent reforms attempted to mitigate the worst of the market failures. These were largely imbalances of power and information that arose between the trusts, the railroads and unscrupulous manufacturers on the one hand, and consumers or small merchants on the other hand during American industrialization.

Drawing on his experiences travelling and ranching in the American West he instituted the Reclamation Service. It funded dams and irrigation for the purpose of bringing arid land into cultivation. 150 national forests as well as five national parks were created under his presidency.

After leaving office, dissatisfied with the direction of the Republican Party under his successor and protege William Howard Taft (1857-1930), and following a failed attempt by Roosevelt to steal the 1912 Republican nomination from Taft, he formed the Progressive Party. This third party split the vote on the right giving the election to the Democrats. Woodrow Wilson (1856-1924) picked up the progressive baton as a Democrat. He made further law related to antitrust and consumer protection and created the Federal Reserve.

"To destroy this invisible Government, to dissolve the unholy alliance between corrupt business and corrupt politics is the first task of the statesmanship of the day. This country belongs to the people. Its resources, its business, its laws, its institutions, should be utilized, maintained, or altered in whatever manner will best promote the general interest." - Theodore Roosevelt

FDR'S NEW DEAL

In response to a stock market panic, failing banks, and unemployment at 24%, Republican Herbert Hoover (1874-1964) raised interest rates, taxes, and tariffs, turning a crisis into a calamity. Franklin Delano Roosevelt (1882-1945), Teddy's *Democratic* nephew, took over the presidency from Hoover when the U.S. was at one of its darkest moments of history.

Falling grain prices and a coincidental drought in the Midwest led to farmer defaults. This put pressure on the Midwestern banks. Some banks defaulted, but worse, confidence in all banks declined, which led to panic spreading throughout the country and an acceleration of bank defaults.

Many FDR Programs Go Too Far

"Unfortunately, the Fed's actions were hesitant and small. In the main, it stood idly by and let the crisis take its course—a pattern of behaviour that was to be repeated again and again during the next two years." - Milton Friedman in Free to Choose

When FDR took power he instituted a series of helpful reforms related to the security markets; deposit insurance; social security for the old and disabled; and public works projects to create jobs for the unemployed. On the other hand, legislation which: implemented compulsory unionization; imposed wage and price controls; and raised bank reserves in the midst of the crisis, were counterproductive for the circumstances and were not supported by the progressive movement of the era.

"Roosevelt's policies were very destructive. Roosevelt's policies made the depression longer and worse than it otherwise would have been." - Milton Friedman

While WWII ended the depression statistically, private activity did not normalize until the market-oriented reforms of the so-called "Do Nothing" 80th (Republican) Congress following the war. While production, by order of government fiat, statistically increased during the war, most of it represented a consumption of wealth. The entire war effort was a massive redirection of capital and labour away from private, productive consumption and investment. While nominal unemployment collapsed, this masked the underlying disinvestment and unemployment in the private sector which re-emerged following the war.

Immediately after the war Democrat Harry S. Truman faced massive worker strikes and runaway inflation. Producers were unwilling to sell grain which remained under price controls. When the Republicans regained veto-proof control of Congress in 1946, they rolled back union abuses with "right to work"; lowered income taxes; and, deregulated commodity prices. Often overriding Truman vetos, these actions are credited with launching the 1950's boom.

15

KENNEDY'S NEW FRONTIER

At the time of John F. Kennedy's (1917-1963) inauguration, the U.S. had been in recession for nine months. He inherited a sluggish economy due to Republican Dwight Eisenhower's (1890-1969) tight post-war money policy. Under the label "New Frontier", Kennedy unleashed every Keynesian tool of government to stimulate the economy with spending.

He expanded unemployment benefits and provided aid for urban housing and transportation. Approved spending was accelerated for the national highway system, hospitals, and rural electrification.

Kennedy's Keynesian Surge and Neo-Liberal Course Correction

Assistance to farmers, Social Security, minimum wages, food for the poor, school milk and lunch programs were increased. A version of the depression Food Stamp Program, cancelled mid-war, was reintroduced. All previously authorized funds were rushed out the door, and states were urged to follow the federal example.

Then he moved on to monetary stimulus. Federally administered housing and small business interest rates were lowered and the Federal Reserve was encouraged to keep rates down through bond purchases. Effective corporate tax rates were reduced. The economy recovered strongly following this double-barrelled fiscal and monetary stimulus.

In the spirit of Teddy Roosevelt, Kennedy successfully went after the American steel industry for price fixing. However, U.S. corporations which were now international, responded by redirecting investment in new plants offshore. The stock market decline accelerated.

He attempted to reduce the top marginal tax rates dramatically (from 91%) but met with resistance from Congress as the economy was already improving.

From John Kennedy's 1962 Economic Club of New York Speech:
"The final and best means of strengthening demand among consumers and business is to reduce the burden on private income and the deterrents to private initiative which are imposed by our present tax system; ... it reduces the financial incentives for personal effort, investment, and risk-taking."

"The Federal Government's most useful role is not to rush into a program of excessive increases in public expenditures, but to expand the incentives and opportunities for private expenditures."

JOHNSON'S WAR ON POVERTY

Lyndon B. Johnson (1908-1973) introduced *The War on Poverty* in 1964. It was part of his *Great Society* initiative inspired by Walter Lippman's book *The Good Society*.

The War on Poverty was in response to a national poverty rate of nineteen percent and the publication of *"The Other America"*, an expose on poverty by Michael Harrington, a member of the Socialist Party.

Johnson Lowers Tax Rates

From humble origins, Johnson worked himself through college. He taught impoverished Mexican-American children in Texas which made an impression on him.

"Our aim is not only to relieve the symptom of poverty, but to cure it and, above all, to prevent it." – Lyndon Johnson

The program assisted the poor with getting access to job training and education and funded the rebuilding of slum areas. FDR-style employment programs were created in impoverished rural areas.

"Poverty must not be a bar to learning and learning must offer an escape from poverty." - Lyndon B. Johnson

Following Kennedy's failed attempt to reduce marginal tax rates from 91% to 65%, Johnson was able to get the top rates cut to 70% in 1965, a move applauded by neoclassical economists. Poverty did decline significantly during the Johnson years, attributed to these lower marginal tax rates and more effective job training and work placement.

Johnson's legislative productivity was massive. He established Medicare and Medicaid, The School Breakfast Program and expanded Social Security. He created NPR, PBS and built the Kennedy Centre. Consumer protection legislation was enacted regarding: automobiles (some say in response to Ralph Nader's book, Unsafe at any Speed); cigarette package labelling; truth in packaging and labelling; meat inspection; and, truth in lending. Environmental legislation was enacted regarding clean water and air, and for protection of species, wildernesses, and historic sites.

"No member of our generation who wasn't a communist or a dropout in the thirties is worth a damn." - Lyndon B. Johnson

REAGAN'S SUPPLY SIDE ECONOMICS

Ronald Reagan (1911-2004) was a neoconservative convert to the Republican Party, having become concerned about: communist influence in the union movement; union power; the relationship between unionism and the Democratic Party; and increasingly "Big Government".

His views came to be known popularly as "Supply Side" economics, drawing on the Chicago School. Milton Friedman, Arthur Laffer (born 1924), and future Federal Reserve chair Alan Greenspan (born 1926, part of Ayn Rand's inner circle), were members of Reagan's Economic Policy Advisory Board.

Reagan Unleashes Neoclassical (Market) Economics on the U.S. Economy

The hypothesis, supported by neoclassical economics (primacy of supply, demand, and free market pricing), was that by merely getting out of people's hair, with less taxes, government spending, and regulation, more enterprise would arise due to society's organic creative energy, guided by Adam Smith's invisible hand, hitherto constrained.

In this way, smaller government would lead to more jobs, higher wages, and cheaper products. This is in contrast to Keynesian redistribution, high taxes, and centralization of decision making. Eventually, the latter reduces the size of the economic pie by distorting prices and resource allocation. It grows public debt, crowding out productive, private investment.

A core hypothesis of supply-siders was that general taxation levels were well past the point of optimal revenue generation on the Laffer Curve. A marginal tax rate reduction was hypothesized to increase overall revenue, which turned out to be true. The Laffer Curve is like climbing a hill, with rising tax rates bringing in rising total tax revenue up to an optimal point, beyond which higher rates bring in declining total tax revenue due to the growing disincentives to risk, effort, work, and investment.

Reagan also adopted Milton Friedman's monetarism. This suggested a decisive contraction of the money supply as his response to the double-digit inflation inherited from Jimmy Carter (born 1924). Consequently, inflation went down sharply from 12.5% to 4.4%, permanently ending the phenomenon of stagflation.

"How do you tell a communist? Well, it's someone who reads Marx and Lenin. And how do you tell an anti-Communist? It's someone who understands Marx and Lenin." - Ronald Reagan

"ENDING WELFARE AS WE KNOW IT"

Reagan's initiatives focused on inflation, public sector unions, and the Cold War. When Bill Clinton (born 1946) assumed the presidency, there remained the task of dealing with a growing perception that the structure of FDR's welfare programming needed reform.

Factors included: the discouragement of marriage and labour force participation of single mothers; activists educating the poor on how to access and manipulate the program; multigenerational dependency; accelerating pressure on state budgets; and circumstances and requirements varying greatly between regions and states, with states demanding reform.

Clinton Cuts Welfare in Half

Clinton's *Temporary Assistance for Needy Families (TANF)* program under the *Personal Responsibility and Work Opportunity Act* was signed into law in 1996, as per his campaign promise to "end welfare as we know it". This transition would be more accurately described as departing from federally designed welfare for single mothers in favour of workfare for men as well as women, irrespective of marital status, customized by state.

TANF was restricted by a lifetime limit of 60 months, or less in some states, and the requirement that the recipient find employment within 24 months of beginning support. Subsidized work opportunity jobs were provided by some states as well as childcare and child health insurance.

Additionally, employers were given tax credits for hiring long-time recipients of welfare. In the years following TANF, welfare caseloads were cut in half and participation in the workforce by recipients increased fourfold.

The earned-income tax credit (EITC), an employment-based version of Milton Friedman's negative income tax idea, first introduced by Gerald Ford in 1975 and enhanced by Reagan, was doubled by Clinton. Most economists believe EITCs are preferable to minimum wages. They are free of the job creation disincentives associated with minimum wages which often require employers to pay more than the productivity of unskilled workers. Minimum wages remove many low-paying first- rung-of-the-ladder job opportunities for the chronically unemployed.

"Work is about more than making a living, as vital as that is. It's fundamental to human dignity, to our sense of self-worth as useful, independent, free people."- Bill Clinton

"I can spend your money better than you can." - Bill Clinton, January 20, 1999

"The most important social welfare program in America is a job." - Newt Gingrich

AMERICAN POLITICAL PARTIES

Following the American Revolution, Alexander Hamilton (1755-1804) organized the Federalist Party, which favoured high tariffs and a strong central government. It was friendly to Britain and the wealthy. In opposition to this was James Madison's (1751-1836) and Thomas Jefferson's (1743-1826) Democratic-Republican Party.

The elitist Federalists faded away and in 1829 the Democratic-Republicans split into Democrats and Whigs. The Democrats supported the primacy of the President over Congress and were free traders, the Whigs taking the opposite view.

Lincoln's Republican Party Launched to Oppose Slavery

In 1854 the Whigs split over the issue of slavery, with the pro-slavery faction merging with the Democrats and the anti-slavery element forming the Republican Party. The Republicans inherited the high tariff policy of the Whigs which remained a central platform plank following the Civil War up to Hoover's very unhelpful Smoot-Hawley Tariff of 1930, the latter which cut trade in half.

Apart from anti-liberal views on tariffs, the emergent Republicans led on most progressive issues such as anti-trust, women's suffrage and going after the corrupt political machines. The failure of the Republicans to prevent and deal with the Great Depression led to the Democrats taking over progressive issues under FDR. Among many other reforms, FDR initiated bilateral (negotiated) tariff reduction in 1934, which continues to this day.

Following WWII and the continuing stagnation of the private sector, the Republicans regained control of Congress. They embraced bilateral tariff reform and otherwise reasserted neoclassical, market-oriented economic policies, while the Democrats retained a relatively Keynesian bias in favour of government institutions and unions.

In the 1960s under Barry Goldwater (1909-1998) and Richard Nixon (1913-1994), the Republicans sought to capture the support of southern whites through the racist "Southern Strategy", which permanently alienated black voters who had historically supported the party of Lincoln.

In the late 20th century the growing political activism and visibility of socially conservative Republicans, opposed to gay marriage and abortion, alienated the entire LBGT community and many socially liberal, but fiscally conservative women. More recently, the unsympathetic speaking points of paleo-conservatives and the conservative media regarding illegal immigration, immigration reform, and amnesty, has alienated the growing Hispanic political constituency.

UPPER CANADA POLITICAL PARTIES

Following the War of 1812, the British Lt. Governors of the Canadas had appointed corrupt and self-serving legislative councils to rule Lower and Upper Canada.

The Family Compact dominated Upper Canada's legislative council, and Lower Canada was ruled by the Chateau Clique, both Tory, meaning: English; Episcopal; royalist; and conservative.

The Tory Family Compact was noted for its elitism and opposition to universal male suffrage. "Family" did not mean relations by marriage, but rather a close brotherhood of Tories attempting to replant the concept of a landed gentry in the colony.

John A. MacDonald, First Prime Minister of Canada

In Upper Canada, the Reform Movement, not formally a party, was led by Irish and American Loyalist elements. Loyalists were immigrant refugee Americans loyal the British crown during the revolution. The Reform Movement was formed in opposition to the Family Compact, ultimately leading to the Upper Canada Rebellion of 1837. The British response to the rebellion was to merge Upper and Lower Canada into the one province of Canada, East (Quebec) and West (Ontario).

Following unification the Canada West Reform movement worked with the relatively radical Canada-East Parti Rouge to form government at various points in the 1840s. By the 1850s the Reform movement had dissipated. Moderates joined with the Tories in 1854 to form a Liberal-Conservative coalition government under the leadership of John A. MacDonald (1815-1891) and Parti Bleu leader George-Etienne Cartier (1814-1873). This alliance ultimately became the Conservative Party.

The agrarian Clear Grits of Southwestern Ontario arose in the late 1840s. The name refers to members being "all sand and no dirt, clear grit all the way through". It advocated universal male suffrage (one man one vote), representation by population, democratic institutions, reductions in government expenditure, the abolition of the Clergy (Land) Reserves and free trade with the United States. It shared many ideas with Thomas Jefferson.

In 1857, the Clear Grits and former left-leaning urban Reformers of Canada West, the Canada East Parti Rouge, and the Liberal parties of the Maritimes formed the Liberal Party of Canada. Their core platform was free trade and provincial rights which the Conservatives at the time opposed.

LOWER CANADA POLITICAL PARTIES

In Lower Canada, the mostly francophone, elected Legislative *Assembly* was frustrated with the anglophone Chateau Clique and the British-appointed Legislative *Council*. This sparked the formation of the *Parti Canadien* in 1806.

It was supported by liberal professionals and small-scale merchants. Their principle goal was to have the Legislative *Council* appointed by the majority party of the elected Legislative *Assembly*, instead of by the Crown-appointed Lt. Governor.

In 1825, the Crown abolished quasi-feudal seigniorial rights in Lower Canada, further infuriating the francophone elite, especially Louis-Joseph Papineau (1786-1871), who sent a list of demands to the Crown. He was the landlord of the Seigneurie de la Petite-Nation and leader of the Parti Canadien since 1815. The following year they took the name *Parti Patriote*, with the more ambitious goal of semi-autonomy.

Joseph Papineau, First Quebec Separatist

The Crown ignored Papineau's demands leading to a call for outright independence, or even joining the U.S. Following the unsuccessful Rebellions of 1837, the party was dissolved by force and leaders were hung or escaped into self-exile.

Following the unification of the Upper and Lower Canada colonies, many exiles, like Papineau, returned after receiving pardons. Papineau sat in Parliament as an independent and Republican, isolated in opposition to monarchism.

He was a signatory of the *Montreal Annexation Manifesto* (1849) which called for joining the U.S. This was at a juncture when U.K. Robert Peele repealed the mercantilist U.K. "Corn (grain) Laws" which had favoured colony trade. The Crown negotiated a short-lived free-trade agreement between Canada and the U.S. to placate the Canadians, but this was rescinded by the Americans when the U.K. took the side of the South during the Civil War.

In 1847, the spirit of reform in the province of Canada East reconstituted itself under the left-wing *Parti Rouge*, adopting the colour of European revolution and socialism, which traces back to the ancient red battle flag signifying "no surrender, to the death." They promoted democratic reform, removing the church from politics, and advocated separation from Canada West. They merged into the Liberal Party of Canada in 1867.

Rivalling the Parti Rouge, the *Parti Bleu* was a *relatively* conservative political group that emerged in 1854, based on the pro-clerical (Roman Catholic Church) views of Louis-Hippolyte Lafontaine. Its name was likely inspired by the dark blue employed by royalist British Tories. They allied with the Tories of Canada West, which formed the basis of the future Conservative Party in 1867.

PROGRESSIVES, SOCIAL CREDIT, CCF & NDP

A decade after the failure of Teddy Roosevelt's Progressive Party, populist farmers, labour, socialists and radical former Liberals cooperated politically in the 1920s under the Progressive movement banner, including briefly forming the Progressive Party of Canada, the first third party to emerge in Parliament.

Upon achieving some electoral momentum federally, actually, the second position in Parliament, the party could not adjust to the disciplines, moderation and compromise required to function as the official opposition, and formally turned down the Governor General's offer!

C. H. Douglas's Social Credit Movement

The movement then split into its constituent parts. Moderates were reabsorbed into the Liberal Party. Socialists, Labour, and some cooperative-oriented farmers eventually formed the explicitly socialist Alberta-based Cooperative Commonwealth Federation (CCF) in 1932, later rebranding itself as the New Democratic Party (NDP) in 1961.

The rural populists, many with social conservative leanings, supported Social Credit in the 1930s based on British engineer C. H. Douglas's (1879–1952) theory that there was a flaw in the economy. The alleged flaw was that consumer demand did not consume the costs of production, and this gap could be closed by distributing free money for people to spend, a primitive version of Keynesian deficit spending.

Keynes agreed that a gap might arise during a rarely occurring liquidity trap such as existed in the depression when everyone was sitting on their hands and money, not lending and not investing in capital equipment. However, Keynes's solution was more along the lines of printing regular money for government spending rather than Douglas's less pragmatic scheme.

Much to its and everyone's surprise, the Social Credit Party rose to power in Alberta with a landslide victory in 1935. However, it was overwhelmed by the details of governing and constrained by the lack of provincial jurisdiction over banks. Against Douglas's advice, under pressure from the party caucus to do something, the leadership issued awkward *prosperity certificates,* which were rejected by Albertans.

Successive Social Credit governments under Ernest Manning, father of Reform Party founder Preston Manning, focused on exploiting the oil windfall in Alberta. Following the ascent of Keynesianism post-war, the problem of under-stimulation of the economy was replaced by chronic, unsustainable, Keynesian over-stimulation.

PROGRESSIVE CONSERVATIVES

While most early Canadian progressives of the 1920s eventually returned to the Liberals or migrated to the Cooperative Commonwealth Federation (CCF), the name itself migrated to the Conservatives due to an anomaly of history.

In 1922, the United Farmers of Manitoba fielded a slate of candidates for the provincial election, hoping to establish a political beachhead in the provincial Parliament. However, they did not even bother to establish a leader as the overall effort was a long shot at best.

Dr. John Braken's Progressive Conservatives

To their surprise, they won the majority of seats in the Manitoba legislature and had to scramble to find a leader. They decided to ask the respected agronomy professor and President of the Manitoba Agricultural College, Dr. John Bracken (1883-1969). He was known by every successful farmer in the province, but had not even run.

Inspired by other 1920s populist agrarian progressives, the group adopted the banner of the Progressive Party of Manitoba, but notably, adopted an ideology of "running government like a business", with non-partisanship. They absolutely rejected the mirror concept of "running business like government", which is socialism.

Bracken led Manitoba for over 20 years and at the beginning of WWII created a comprehensive wartime coalition that included all political parties. In 1942, based on his successes in Manitoba, he was recruited to lead the federal Conservative Party in Ottawa.

He accepted the invitation on one condition: the party was to add "Progressive" to its name.

Provincial organizations followed suit over time. He was not able to lead the party to power and otherwise did not leave much of a mark, other than the name change. It is speculated that as a westerner, he was perceived to be an outsider to the Central Canadian power structure.

The significance of *Progressive* Conservatism is that is supports the view that progressivism is not equal to socialism or Robin Hood Liberalism. Rather, its core historical meaning suggests *pragmatic reform and experimentation, trained on problems dominating society at a given moment.*

PRESTON MANNING'S REFORM PARTY

In 1987, western populism reemerged at the federal level as the fiscal, and sometimes socially conservative Reform Party.

It was founded by Preston Manning (born 1942), the son of former Alberta Social Credit Premier Ernest Manning. It was in protest of: Brian Mulroney's handling of the economy; the introduction of G.S.T.; and, the emphasis on bringing Quebec into the constitution.

Unfortunately, socially conservative views gave encouragement to expressions of out-of-date, socially unprogressive values by some Members of Parliament, alienating many urban and Eastern voters.

Preston Manning eventually resigned due to his alarm over vote-splitting with the Progressive

Manning Divides the Right

Conservatives, which was keeping the Liberals in power. He engineered the formation of the Alliance Party in 2001, but lost the leadership to socially conservative Stockwell Day.

Completion of the merging of the right was stalled by Red Tory Joe Clark's intransigence, leader of the legacy Progressive Conservative Party. The Alliance struggled in opposition under Stockwell Day.

Authentically neoconservative Steven Harper (former Reach for the Top contestant), started out as a Liberal in his university years. He broke with the Pierre Trudeau Liberals because of the National Energy Program, which was understood by westerners to be a wealth transfer from the west to the east. He later broke with Brian Mulroney's Progressive Conservatives over a perceived lack of fiscal discipline, and the slow walking of the repeal of the National Energy Program.

Harper was recruited to be Reform's Chief Policy Officer under Preston Manning. He was the Chief of Staff of the first Reform MP, Deborah Grey, going on to eventually winning a seat for himself in Parliament and ousting Stockwell Day to become the leader of the Alliance in 2002.

It was finally under Harper that the party was able to move forward politically and break the choke-hold the Naturally Governing Party, the Liberals, had on voters since Brian Mulroney. With the cooperation of Peter MacKay, who became Progressive Conservative leader in 2003, they fulfilled Manning's original vision of installing the first Western-based leader since Diefenbaker, forming the modern Conservative Party under Harper's leadership.

CHAPTER 4 – A BEDTIME FABLE ON CAPITALISM

THE BASIC HISTORICAL STORY OF WORK, TRADE, INVENTION, ENTREPRENEURSHIP, EMPLOYMENT, THRIFT, SAVINGS, CAPITAL, FIRMS AND MONEY.

"A professor must have a theory as a dog must have fleas." - H. L. Mencken

ONCE UPON A TIME, IN THE WEST

The starting point of economic evolution is a
tribal unit of naked pre-humans roaming
around scavenging for edible things to eat.
There are no tools nor stores of consumption
goods. This is life at the animal level, with no
actual economics to analyze, in the
conventional sense.

At some point, someone encounters a quantity
of nuts that is more than the tribe can eat, and
those get carried back to the cave or campsite.
This is the genesis of savings, as a flow, and
wealth as a stock, in the form of a consumable.
Such wealth may be held by an individual,
maybe the chief, or may be held as community
property.

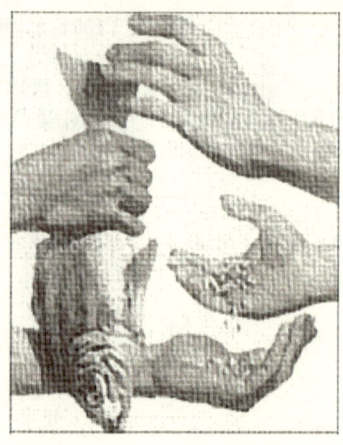

Humans Discover Trade

Under tribal community property economics, there is little personal incentive to
find surpluses of nuts as what you find will mostly be consumed by someone else
and there is little incentive to conserve nuts, because what you don't eat will be
eaten by someone else. From each according to their ability, to each, or the chief,
according to their need.

This is why there is little sustainable wealth creation under community property or
community-earning arrangements. Case in point, America's Pilgrims started out
under a community property communist model, but they immediately starved. They
subsequently instituted private property.

At some point tribes discover the right of the individual or family biological unit to
own property. Under this arrangement, the family breadwinner(s) is incented to find
nuts for himself and his family as well as conserve them for future personal use.

Mr. Nutfinder has a passion for finding nuts, gets really good at it. One day Mr.
Nutfinder is sitting on his pile of nuts and he sees his neighbour Mr. Figfinder
sitting on a pile of figs. He is tired of eating nuts all the time, and the other guy is
tired of eating figs all the time, and they discover trade.

They probably start out trading one nut for one fig but at some point Mr. Nutfinder
considers the fact that he has to walk twice as far to find nuts, and they are harder to
carry back to the camp, and he has a smaller pile of nuts than the pile of figs of Mr.
Figfinder. So he asks for two figs for one nut, and the other fellow grudgingly
accepts.

WHAT A TOOL!

So that is savings, wealth and trade, but we do not yet have capitalism, as at this point tools do not enter the equation, they being tool-less hunters and gatherers in our greatly simplified model of economic pre-history.

The first tool might have been a conveniently shaped and sized stone for shelling nuts, which for our fable is called a Nutstone. Initially, Mr. Nutfinder probably found the first such stone, and one day, perhaps one of his sons becomes especially good at finding such stones, and he adopts the name, Mr. NutStonefinder.

Humans Discover Tools (Capital)

He sits on his pile of nutstones and trades them for nuts and figs on market day in the tribal village. This is the birth of non-consumable capital. All wealth that is non-consumable is a form of tool or facilitation for creating, storing or transporting a consumable.

So, here we have people specializing in finding and processing consumables, as well as acquiring processing tools. An entire multi-generational family is likely participating in each speciality, not dissimilar to the early 20th-century family farm.

One day, Mr. Nutfinder's second son, Mr. Nutsheller, has a lineup of nutfinders and figfinders outside his tent ready to trade for shelled nuts, but he can't keep up with demand.

He has piles of unshelled nuts and plenty of nutstones from his brother Mr. Nutstonefinder, but no extra children, spouses or parents available to actually shell nuts, and he hates seeing customers quit the line to go to the unscrupulous nutshellers across the street.

Mr. Figfinder cannot keep his large family busy enough or fed. He is good enough at finding figs, but he simply has too many offspring to keep them all busy finding, transporting or selling figs, or is getting too old to bother.

He proposes to his busy neighbour, "how about you take my son who thinks he is too smart for figfinding, and teach him how to shell nuts, maybe pay him eight nuts per hour?" This is the birth of the employer, employee relationship. Win, win. Not everyone wants to work for the family firm; not everyone is suited to self-employment.

ALL THAT GLITTERS IS GOLD

Mr. Nutsheller is so busy trading shelled nuts for everything his neighbours have to trade, that he has little time to eat all of his food surpluses. Piles of consumable stuff start piling up outside of his tent.

Animals and neighbours steal his stuff so he trades these various consumables for things that are small, valuable and non-perishable, like gold and silver, that he can bury under his tent. He eventually retires from nutcrushing, and is simply known as Mr. Stashes-it-under-the-tent.

Micronesian Rai Stone Currency

His son, Mr. Nutsheller II, instead of accumulating small valuable things under his tent, rather, spends most of his growing surplus on even more helpers to scale up his work tent. To keep these employees productive, he provides a nutstone for each of them.

Or its the other way around, first comes the tool, then the workers to animate the tools. Tools make workers more productive, more valuable, justifying higher wages. Its a symbiotic relationship.

At some point, they figure out how to move beyond barter to trading for standardized units of gold, eventually supervised by the state as gold coin. Nuts are traded for gold and gold is traded for nutstones, nuts and nutsheller workers.

Mr. NutStonefinder retires and just makes a living from offering NutStones for rent, becoming known as Mr. Nutstonelender, which is the intuitive beginning of actual capitalism, the trading of capital, or tools.

At some point, he sells all his NutStones for gold coin, builds a fortress to house it, and rather lends gold coin for interest, and then gold borrowers take the gold and buy nutstones at the market. They shell nuts and sell them, and make payments to him now known as Mr. Goldlender.

As he already has a fortress for his gold, others ask to deposit their accumulated gold and market-day profits in his guarded fortress. He lends their gold out for an interest rate and pays a portion of this to the depositors as an incentive to attract deposits.

This is the birth of banking. At some point, the original banker would fade from the enterprise and be fully funded by depositors.

SHARE AND SHARE ALIKE

Mr. Nutsheller does exceptionally well hiring ten ambitious offspring of his neighbours. He figures out cost-saving efficiencies and cuts the price of shelled nuts so that even his poorest neighbours can afford them, selling out early every morning. He thinks, if only I could double my size with ten more nutshellers!

Early Traders Under the Buttonwood Tree on Wall Street

Mr. Goldlender, who initially lent him the gold to buy the first ten nutstones, won't lend him any more gold to buy nutstones, so he hatches a different plan. Rather, he offers his wealthy friends, who have gold in Mr. Goldlender's bank, a share of the future profits of his company. There is the likelihood that they would make much more money than the paltry interest that Mr. Goldlender gives them at the bank, directly owning a share of the enterprise and cutting out the banker middleman.

An advantage for Mr. Nutsheller is that he can pay these "shareholders" out of profits when times are good, which is called "dividends," meaning profit "to be divided." By comparison, a gold loan from Mr. Goldlender has a fixed payback payment with interest, regardless of how sales are going. It entails the risk that the bank might foreclose on his nutshelling tools and nut inventory, as well as his grass hut, if he is unlucky or if there is a temporary drop in sales.

Manhatten shareholders started trading shares among themselves under a buttonwood tree on Wall Street. This was the genesis of the New York Stock Exchange. At some point, bankers started giving out promissory notes backed by gold, instead of actual gold. It was more convenient, and eventually, governments took over this role of issuing these notes. These notes became paper money backed by gold at Fort Knox. The final step was to delink the national currency from gold backing and rather have it backed by the faith and credit of the government.

The point of this fable is that *tools animate the prosperity of workers*, and *tools arise from the savings of savers*, and *many tools arise from the savings of super savers, A.K.A., "the rich."* Any society which does not appropriately appreciate the role of super savers will find tools (A.K.A. capital) to be more scarce, and consequently, the workers will be less productive, limiting what firms can pay them. The other point is that the creative class of the entrepreneur is the goose that lays the golden egg of employment opportunity, creating jobs and new industries where there were none, bringing workers together with tools. No productive, tax generating job is created, without an entrepreneur.

DON'T BITE THE HAND

The thing is, if you are not trained at finding nuts or capitalized for shelling nuts on your own, your next best opportunity is to rent out your time and skills to someone who can provide training, tools, shelter and buyers. The "entre-preneur" is the "between-taker", or "he who undertakes", who puts all the pieces together, for those who cannot do so themselves through self-employment.

The Necessity of Tough Love For the Motivationally Challenged

Failing that, your next best opportunity might be digging for worms or something and starving. Or worse, moving into your mother's basement. What this illustrates is the co-dependence between the employed and employers. "The Man" is not your oppressor, "The Man" is your partner, and sometimes your rescuer!

Like the loving parent, football coach or boot camp drill sergeant, this sometimes uncomfortable pressure of supervision is love, though indeed often a "tough" love, and sometimes more gratuitously tough than love. *Those who's egos are such that they cannot submit to the uncomfortable pressure of the caring but firm parent, the demanding coach with high expectations, the strict supervisor, they are on a bad path in life, with greatly reduced opportunity and choices.*

One option is self-employment and entrepreneurship, for the courageous, though even there, there is the albeit more diffuse pressure of the demanding client, and a trap of poverty for the unmotivated, the unlucky or the undercapitalized.

The other important relationship that is undervalued in society is the role of the super saver, Mr. Goldlender. *All savings are postponed consumption*, reflecting a decision to trade nuts for gold, and gold for tools, instead of figs to eat. Consider the Stanford Marshmallow Experiment. A small percentage of humanity has this unnatural propensity to live below their means, sometimes on a grand scale, sometimes with one generation building on the postponed consumption of the previous generation, in a virtuous cycle.

All such wealth that arises in a free society, through free exchange, is a reflection of this unusual self-control and willingness to delay gratification. The rich are truly different. It may drift into the pathology of miserliness, love of money, but even this actually serves the borrowing entrepreneur and worker in need of tools. It increases the supply of capital that enables enterprise and elevates the productivity of workers, their value in the labour marketplace, raising what they can *sustainably* be paid by firms.

CHAPTER 5 – HISTORY OF MARKET ECONOMICS

"Everyone sits in the prison of his own ideas; he must burst it open, and that in his youth, and so try to test his ideas on reality." - Albert Einstein

"The curious task of economics is to demonstrate to men how little they really know about what they imagine they can design." - Friedrich A. Hayek

"The champions of socialism call themselves progressives, but they recommend a system which is characterized by rigid observance of routine and by a resistance to every kind of improvement. They call themselves liberals, but they are intent upon abolishing liberty. They call themselves democrats, but they yearn for dictatorship. They call themselves revolutionaries, but they want to make the government omnipotent. They promise the blessings of the Garden of Eden, but they plan to transform the world into a gigantic post office. Every man but one a subordinate clerk in a bureau."
— Ludwig von Mises, Bureaucracy

ADAM SMITH, FATHER OF ECONOMICS

Adam Smith (1723 -1790), a witness to the birth of the British Industrial Revolution, the father of economics, was a Scottish path breaker of political economy who wrote the *Wealth of Nations* (1776), marking the beginning of modern economics. Smith, a lifelong bachelor, reportedly told a friend that he wrote the book "to fill the time."

Smith established classical free-market economic theory, outlining how rational self-interest and competition can lead to economic prosperity. To that end he argued, free trade, allocation by price and not by king or government, and division of labour, are key to producing wealth.

Smith, a Lifelong Bachelor, Writes the Wealth of Nations to Pass the Time

The greater the access to markets through unfettered trade and access to water transportation, the greater the opportunity for division of labour. With the division of labour, money and exchange are required for each person to fulfil their needs.

He opposed the mercantile system of promoting exports and using tariffs to resist imports for the purpose of building up gold reserves, observing that a nation's wealth lay not in its gold reserves, but rather in its productive capacity.

Smith was also a "classical" progressive at heart. He was very concerned about the asymmetry of negotiating power between paycheck to paycheck labourers and deep-pocketed employers. He was also concerned about the tendency of industry owners to collude on product pricing. He supported public education for poor adults.

"The subjects of every state ought to contribute towards the support of the government, as nearly as possible, in proportion to their respective abilities; that is, in proportion to the revenue which they respectively enjoy under the protection of the state." Adam Smith

"...by directing that industry in such a manner as its produce may be of the greatest value, he intends only his own gain, and he is in this, as in many other cases, led by an *invisible hand* to promote an end which was no part of his intention... By pursuing his own interest, he frequently promotes that of the society more effectually than when he really intends to promote it." (*Wealth of Nations* Book 4, Chapter 2)

It is said former U.K. Prime Minister Margaret Thatcher carried a copy of *Wealth of Nations* in her handbag.

ADAM SMITH'S INVISIBLE HAND

The gap between the entrepreneur's offer of employment or goods, and the next best offer available is a "welfare benefit" to the employee or the customer. This is econo-speak for the authentic alchemy of creating wealth out of thin air.

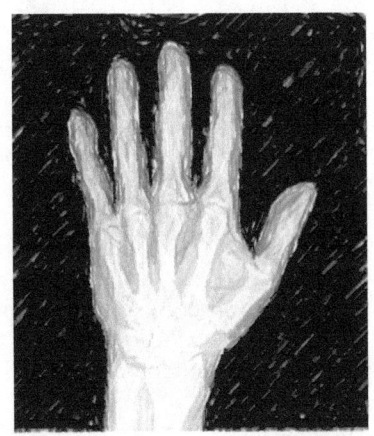

Similar to the man with ten nuts and his neighbour with 10 figs, both are better off, wealthier when they exchange 5 figs for five nuts.

The entrepreneur experiences a welfare benefit as well. This is the gap between the value that that customer or employee provides, versus the next best offer. This is the lower price that the employer would have to offer in the absence of that customer's demand or the lower quality of

Individuals Pursuing their Self Interest Produces Prosperity

employee that is the next person on the list. It's a win-win in both directions, and this is the basis of utility or wealth creation, in free-choice markets.

The entrepreneur provides this benefit, entirely unintentionally. It is one part of the magic of Adam Smith's mysterious invisible hand.

"I find myself more and more relying for a solution of our problems on the invisible hand which I tried to eject from economic thinking twenty years ago" John Maynard Keynes, at the end of his life.

At each price point of the market, except one, there is a surplus of goods provided by suppliers, or a shortage of goods, relative to consumer demand. There is only one price, at any given moment, where the quantities of goods supplied matches the quantity of goods that will be purchased. Price, tells all of the market participants where they stand according to the aggregate market.

If you are a consumer or purchaser and the value to you of a unit is less than the market price, you will not be buying. If the value of the unit to you is greater than the market price, you will be buying. The gap between what you pay for a unit, and its value to you, is an increase in your wealth, or utility, in econospeak.

The wealth of a society is created through free choice and cooperation. Each partner seeks out their highest best use to earn money from selling their service on a market, and the highest best use for their earned money when purchasing goods or services.

MENGER, AUSTRIAN SCHOOL FOUNDER

Carl Menger (1840-1921) was noble born the son of a wealthy Austrian lawyer and heiress. While trained in the law and some economics, he initially worked as a journalist reporting on market news, where he noticed discrepancies between Adam Smith's classical cost-based explanation of prices, versus market action.

Rather, he was the first to assert that prices are determined by the marginal value and marginal cost of the last unit produced and sold.

The first slice of pizza has greater value than the 20th, for a given customer, and producing the first ten pizzas has a lower cost than producing the last ten pizzas on a given evening, in an industry operating close to capacity.

Menger Launches the Academic War Against Socialism

The current pizza offered is priced on its value to the customer in combination with its cost to the producer. Further, labour is valued based on the value of this production to the producer. Also, all trade is beneficial to both producer and buyer. Middlemen and entrepreneurs facilitate achieving these benefits of trade.

He also explained that money organically arose, as an example of "spontaneous order," to overcome the awkwardness of barter, initially employing something widely accepted, such as cattle, then evolving toward precious metals.

He returned to school to specialize in political economy, resulting in him Publishing *Principles of Economics* (1871), establishing him as the father of the Austrian School, rapidly rising to Chair of Economic Theory at the University of Vienna by age 33.

He opposed the Historical School which dominated German thought. German opinion leaders would refer to Menger's views derisively as the "Austrian School". He directly attacked their views with *The Errors of Historicism in German Economics* (1884).

Unlike the Austrian School, the Historical School documented in great detail economic phenomena as history, devoid of universal principles or laws. Consequently, with no theoretical position, it regressed to being a pragmatic apologism for Bismark's welfare state and socialism. Menger asserted that there were indeed universal principles and laws of economics and that these observations had inconvenient implications for socialists and statists.

"There is no better means of reducing a fallacious variety of thought to absurdity than to let it live itself out completely." - Carl Menger

LUDVIG VON MISES, AUSTRIAN VOICE IN THE WILDERNESS

Ludvig von Mises (1881-1973) was born into Austrian nobility and the intellectual elite. He was a supporter and populizer of the Austrian School, founded by Carl Menger.

His classical liberal views (freedom from limitation by the state) were so uncompromising in the face of growing socialist, fascist and statist thinking, and growing antisemitism in Austria, he was unable to achieve an academic post. However, he led an influential seminar out of his governmental office for many years, attended by F.A. Hayek, a government subordinate at the time.

Von Mises Revives the Academic War Against Statism and Socialism

He is credited with saving Austria from communism following WWI. He convinced the newly elected Marxist President Karl Seitz to abandon that path in a legendary all-night discussion. Following senior governmental and NGO posts in Austria and his first academic position in Switzerland, he fled to America and New York City to escape the advancing Nazis, fearing an invasion of Switzerland. He held an unpaid position at New York University until his retirement, which was funded by Lawrence W. Fertig (1898-1986), an American advertising executive and libertarian journalist.

Mise's contribution is recognized to be more prophetic than providing new art to economic theory. His was a jarring, early, persistent and often inflexible voice speaking up in favour of free markets. This when the intellectual tide was going the opposite way. His views not only formed the basis of Hayek's work, but as well, von Mises and Hayek influenced Milton Friedman through the Mont Pellerin Society.

Human Action: A Treatise on Economics, is considered to be his magnum opus which asserts that all progress arises from profit, which reflects the value consumers put on products and services. Profit is calculated from prices, sales, and costs. Without prices, there can be no calculation, and hence, no progress.

"Socialism substitutes the sovereignty of a dictator, or committee of dictators, for the sovereignty of the consumers." - L. von Mises

"Inequality of wealth and incomes is an essential feature of the market economy. It is the implement that makes the consumers supreme in giving them the power to force all those engaged in production to comply with their orders. It forces all those engaged in production to the utmost exertion in the service of the consumers. It makes competition work. He who best serves consumers, profits most and accumulates riches." - L. von Mises

F. A. HAYEK, MAYNARD KEYNES' FREE MARKET NEMESIS

F. A. Hayek (1899-1992) was born into an academic and wealthy Austrian family, exhibiting prodigy abilities in many fields from an early age. His initial formal studies yielded a doctorate in law which was followed by a doctorate in political economy.

Having established himself as the Austrian School leader of this generation, he was recruited to the London School of Economics to balance out the statist influence of Keynes. He became a British citizen during the Nazi occupation of Austria. He debated Keynes privately and publicly until Keynes' death.

Hayek's War on Keynesianism

Hayek was responsible for several key publications in defence of classical liberalism and libertarianism that had anticipated the eventual global shift away from socialism and central planning, earning him a Nobel for economics late in life.

Hayek was the first to hypothesize that the cause of the boom and bust business cycle was government manipulation of the money supply, rather than some fault of capitalism. He also established the argument that socialism, and even more so, communism, inevitably led to totalitarian coercion of the population.

His book, "The Road to Serfdom", was banned in the Soviet Union. This built on L. Von Mises's earlier work, and Hayek, with Friedman, was also a founding member of the Mont Pellerin Society. Hayek reluctantly wrote the book, having time on his hands during WWII. The British Government would not hire him for the war effort due to his Austrian ethnicity.

Significantly, he explained that a free market price was the only effective way to communicate market conditions to all the participants. Free markets create an organic, spontaneous order to commerce. *He reframed socialism as a question of practical possibility, rather than a question of ethics.*

Hayek adopted the label "libertarian", given that the term liberal had been adopted by socialistic left-leaning elements. However, like Adam Smith, Hayek was no Social Darwinist, writing: "There is no reason why in a free society government should not assure to all, protection against severe deprivation in the form of an assured minimum income, or a floor below which nobody need descend."

SCHUMPETER ON ENTREPRENEURSHIP

In old French, the verb *entreprende* had a meaning of "to undertake or manage".

Early political economist Richard Cantillon (1680-1734), a French-speaking Irishman, first used it as a term of economics. It refers to anyone who at some risk, bought or produced at cost, and sold at another uncertain price, to maximize a financial return, such as farmers and the self- employed.

Jean Baptiste Say (1767-1832) employed the term as "one who undertakes an enterprise, especially a contractor, acting as an intermediary between labour and capital," seeing the entrepreneur, more as a planner/manager than a risk taker.

Schumpeter Identifies the Missing Link of Entrepreneurship

Joseph Schumpeter (1883-1950) more fully launched the theory of the entrepreneur asserting that *entrepreneurs are drivers of change, long-term economic growth, and progress in society through "the gale of creative destruction."* Israel Kirzner later proposed that most innovation is incremental within existing firms, and is not necessarily "destructive" of entrenched firms.

Schumpeter further identified that entrepreneurial innovation actually shifts the production possibility curve to a higher level. Contrary to Baptiste, he believed it was the capitalist who bore the capital risk of an enterprise, not the entrepreneur. In disagreement, Frank Knight and Peter Drucker pointed out that the entrepreneur risks their financial security. They normally have skin in the game through a personal stake in an uncertain venture.

William Jack Baumol (1922-), like Schumpeter, asserted that microeconomic theory was missing a formal treatment of the entrepreneur as the engine of innovation. In response, he offered the book *"The Microtheory of Innovative Entrepreneurship"* as a first formal effort in this regard.

Did this missing element in economics support statist, anti-entrepreneurial, so-called "progressive" policies in the past? Interestingly, Schumpeter predicted that capitalism would eventually collapse due to rising: intellectual opposition to capitalism; "labourism"; and "liberal capitalism," which would degrade the creative destruction of innovative entrepreneurship. Britain's *Winter of Discontent* was evidence that this prediction was coming true.

"Entrepreneurial profit is the expression of the value of what the entrepreneur contributes to production." – Schumpeter

GEORGE SOROS, NEOCLASSICAL CONTRARIAN

Gyorgy Schwartz (born 1930) was renamed Soros, which is Esperanto for "soar" when his Esperantist writer-father changed his name to downplay their Jewish ethnicity leading up to WWII.

Following the war, Soros moved to London where he obtained a Ph.D. in philosophy, but struggled to earn a living. He persevered to get a start in banking and was eventually given his break by a fellow Hungarian, learning arbitrage, which took him to New York.

Worth an estimated $24.5 billion, Forbes ranked him the sixteenth wealthiest person in the U.S. in 2015. In 1992 he infamously "broke the Bank of England", making a billion dollars shorting the pound. Paul Krugman said on Soros..."there really are investors who not only move money in

Soros, the Charles Koch of the Left

anticipation of a currency crisis, but actually do their best to trigger that crisis for fun and profit. These new actors on the scene do not yet have a standard name; my proposed term is 'Soroi'."

Drawing from his experiences with the markets, he developed his theory of *reflexivity* which describes a market state of participant belief and reaction, moving away from standard neoclassical economic equilibrium due to unhelpful feedback loops. The 2008 crisis has drawn attention to his theory.

He asserts that irrational *reflexive* phenomena, such as market bubbles, are market failures that necessitate government intervention, and that pervasive Chicago School "*market fundamentalism*" resists this necessary reform.

Soros is a proponent of *Open Society*, which asserts that civilization progresses from tribal, traditional, and authoritarian "closed" societies, toward tolerant, transparent "open" societies, a term conceived by Henri Bergson and developed by Karl Popper, Soros' mentor in graduate school.

To this end, he funded many open society movements in Eastern Europe preceding the fall of the Berlin wall, with these activities currently spanning Asia and Africa. His Open Society groups are banned in the Soviet Union and many other countries. In the U.S. he supports drug decriminalization and pro-euthanasia campaigns and was deeply opposed to Bush and the "War on Terror". He is co-chairman of a Hillary Clinton super PAC. In 2014, Open Society foundations spent $827 million worldwide.

Soros is criticized from the left for being a pro-capitalist neoliberal, notwithstanding his criticism of market fundamentalism. From the right, he is accused of working toward a unitary global government.

DE SOTO POLAR ON PROPERTY RIGHTS

Hernando de Soto Polar (born 1941) is a Peruvian economist who writes and consults on the importance of property rights.

As a Peruvian diplomat at the time of the 1948 coup, his father chose to exile his family to Switzerland where de Soto was educated in economics. Following an early career as an economist and consultant, he returned to Peru, and in 1979 established *The Institute for Liberty and Democracy* which promotes property rights in developing countries.

De Soto Polar Revolutionizes Third World Development

This arose out of living part of his life in two systems, one with strong property rights, in the West, and one with few property rights for the common person, in Peru, which produces very different results regarding wealth and the wellbeing of the common person.

De Soto convinced then-president Fujimori to move from Keynesian to neoliberal approaches. Neoliberalism is an international term for a shift toward economic liberalism. Neoconservatism has recently become unfairly associated with Republican American promotion of democracy internationally. Fujimori gave property title to 1.2 million squatter families, and permitted 380,000 black market firms to enter the formal economy. GDP per capita increased over 500% in subsequent years.

The de Soto style reforms were copied in many other developing nations. In 2004 he was awarded the *Milton Friedman Prize for Advancing Liberty*, and in 2010 he was awarded the *Hayek Medal*. He is a member of the Mont Pelerin Society. His books include *The Other Path: The Invisible Revolution in the Third Word* (1989), and *The Mystery of Capital: Why Capitalism Triumphs in the West and Fails Everywhere Else.*

From the latter work: "Without an integrated formal property system, a modern market economy is inconceivable. Had the advanced nations of the West not integrated all representations [property titles] into one standardized property system and made it accessible to all, they could not have specialized and divided labour to create the expanded market network and capital that have produced their present wealth. The inefficiencies of non-Western markets have a lot to do with the fragmentation of their property arrangements and the unavailability of standard representations."

STEVEN LEVITT'S FREAKONOMICS ON INCENTIVES

University of Chicago Economist Steven Levitt (born 1967), with journalist Stephen Dubner, (born 1963) is the creator of the Freakonomics publishing franchise, including the best-selling *Freakonomics* (the book and film), *SuperFreakonomics,* and *Think Like a Freak.*

Freakonomics Brings Economics to the People

His core point is that economics, human behaviour and civilization for that matter, is largely about incentives. His significance is that he delivers economics to a popular audience by making it fun and interesting.

"An incentive is a bullet, a key: an often tiny object with astonishing power to change a situation" *Freakonomics*

He demonstrates the power of incentives through examining cheating by Sumo wrestlers when one opponent really needs a win to retain their status, when a loss would have no impact on the other competitor.

His most controversial assertion is that liberal abortion laws not only correlate to but as well, caused, lower crime rates, by reducing the number of unwanted children. He also looks into the long-term impact of giving a child a culturally black first name.

In *SuperFreakonomics*, they controversially wade into responses to global warming beyond the popular and arguably politically impractical focus on CO2 reduction. He examines the role of competition in many contexts, such as free premarital sex driving down the wages of prostitutes; and, the cost-benefit of terrorism.

In *Think Like a Freak*, the direction is away from economics and turns toward removing prejudice, seeing situations naively, and applying out-of-the-box thinking.

Think Like a Freak Quotes:
"Don't listen to what people say; watch what they do."

"But as history clearly shows, most people, whether because of nature or nurture, generally put their own interests ahead of others.' This doesn't make them bad people; it just makes them human."

"When people don't pay the true cost of something, they tend to consume it inefficiently."

CARROTS AND STICKS

Every action of structured and predictable compassion on the part of an entity, be it a government, an NGO or a wealthy parent spoiling a young adult, sets up an incentive for more of the behaviour that generated the need for assistance in the first place. Rewarding failure creates an incentive for more failure.

If there is a Golden Rule of economics, the observation from which everything flows, it is that humans respond to incentives, sometimes weakly, sometimes strongly.

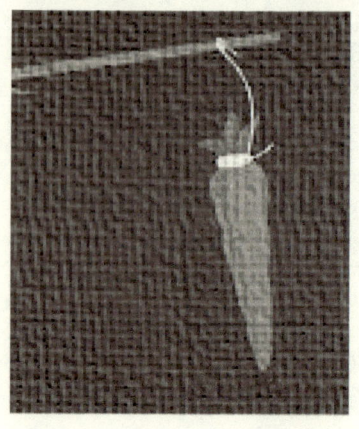

People Respond to Incentives

Incentives take many forms. There are moral incentives, arising from the drive for self-esteem or for the approval or admiration of others. There are coercive physical or financial penalty incentives under the law and natural incentives that relate to biological or mental impulses.

There appears to be a belief that all the stuff at Walmart simply appears like magic. There is no appreciation for the role of inventors, innovators, angel investors, new business founders, and creative managers. As well there is the role of the workers, the sales force and so on, and the fundamental reality that all of them down the line respond to, are primarily driven by incentives.

Virtually all government interference in these organic incentive processes will have profound impacts over time, distorting the allocation of effort, most certainly reducing the wealth of a society.

"Call it what you will, incentives are what get people to work harder." - Nikita Khrushchev, Premier of the Soviet Union, 1958-1964.

"The system that enables the most people to earn the most success is free enterprise, by matching up people's skills, interests, and abilities. In contrast, redistribution simply spreads money around. Even worse, it attenuates the ability to earn success by perverting economic incentives." - Arthur C. Brooks

"I think the problem with schools is not too many incentives but too few. Because of tenure, teachers' unions, and the fact that teachers generally aren't observed in their classrooms, they can do whatever they want in class." - Steven Levitt

"Are people innately altruistic?" is the wrong kind of question to ask. People are people, and they respond to incentives. They can nearly always be manipulated--for good or ill--if only you find the right levers. - Levitt & Dubner, "Superfreakonomics."

LOMBORG ON COST-BENEFIT

One of the most controversial multidisciplinary writers on the current scene and in the public eye is Political Scientist Bjorn Lomborg of Denmark. He is somewhat the mirror image of Al Gore.

Lomborg, in 1998, the director of the Danish Environmental Assessment Institute, shocked by the litany of hysteria and lack of empiricism driving environmental issues, authored the international best-seller, "*The Sceptical Environmentalist: Measuring the Real State of the World*".

He firstly asks the question, what is the true state of the world, based on the data?

"When thinking about the future, it is fashionable to be pessimistic. Yet the evidence

Lomborg Enrages the Environmentalist Movement

unequivocally belies such pessimism. Over the past centuries, humanity's lot has improved dramatically - in the developed world, where it is rather obvious, but also in the developing world, *where life expectancy has more than doubled in the past 100 years*." - Bjorn Lomborg

He reassures the reader that things are not as bad as popular media, or the environmental, industrial complex suggests in their "Litany of Doom and Gloom." He secondly asks a question: regarding the measurable problems of the world, and the available or promising practical solutions, where do we get the best bang for the buck, applying the fundamental tool of cost-benefit analysis?

He offers this in place of the status quo, which is attention and funding being driven toward wasteful projects applied to questionable problems, albeit problems that have a well-funded lobby machine. Reaction to his book was polarized between the silent sympathetic minority and the apoplectic environmental community, which launched a vicious campaign to prevent publication of the book in English.

Based on the controversy the Danish publication garnered, the American version was subjected to extraordinary measures in peer review before publication. The publisher encouraged critics to submit a rebuttal book, without success.

What followed from this was a series of conferences beginning in 2004 with a wider-lens focus on global problems, utilizing cost-benefit analysis, managed by Lomborg's Copenhagen Consensus Centre. The results of the cost-benefit analysis point to greater attention, concern and investment in micro-nutrients, immunization and deworming of children in poor nations, rather than CO_2 reduction, by way of example.

KIRZNER ON ECONOMIC SCIENCE DENIAL

"The phenomenon of economic ignorance is so widespread, and its consequences so frightening, that the objective of reducing that ignorance becomes a goal invested with independent moral worth." Israel Kirzner (born 1933).

Kirzner is a current-day New York University professor, a former student of, assistant to, and current expert on, Ludwig von Mises and his thinking, as well as entrepreneurship.

Kirzner claims that he chose Von Mises as his mentor solely on the fact that he had more books in his office than any other professor.

Kirzner Raises the Alarm Against Economic Ignorance

He soon discovered that the economics profession considered Von Mises and Hayek to be the last of a dead school of thought.

In his book, *Competition and Entrepreneurship* (1973), he expounds on the essential role of the entrepreneur, an element missing in neoclassical theory's emphasis on perfect competition, which ignores the question of who or what force brings a market into equilibrium.

Kirzner is also known for his work on the institutional prerequisites necessary for entrepreneurship to flourish and create wealth, supporting De Soto Polar's views.

In *Discovery, Capitalism, and Distributive Justice* (1989), he explains the creative role of the entrepreneur, who creates new products and wealth that is of value to customers. Through this he documents the ethical justification for rewarding the entrepreneur with profits for his efforts.

Of note, Kirzner is the current-day leader of the Austrian School while also serving as Rabbi of the congregation he inherited from his father.

Kirzner Quotes:

"The essential quality of a market system, contrary to popular thinking, is not that it promotes greed; but rather, that it renders greed harmless."

"The competitive market, Hayek showed us, is a discovery process, in which society discovers what options are feasible and how important they are."

CHAPTER 7 - THRIFT, SAVINGS, CAPITALISTS

"All the political angst and moral melodrama about getting 'the rich' to pay 'their fair share' is part of a big charade. This is not about economics, it is about politics."
- Thomas Sowell

"Back in the thirties we were told we must collectivize the nation because the people were so poor. Now we are told we must collectivize the nation because the people are so rich." - William F. Buckley, Jr.

"I don't have a problem with guilt about money. The way I see it is that my money represents an enormous number of claim checks on society. It is like I have these little pieces of paper that I can turn into consumption. ...I don't use very many of those claim checks. There's nothing material I want very much. And I'm going to give virtually all of those claim checks to charity when my wife and I die. - Warren Buffett (born 1930).

When the unusual circumstance arises that a person does not consume their legally and fairly earned wages, savings is deemed to have occurred. Money in the bank, justly earned, is postponed consumption, nothing more, nothing less. Not the spoils of exploitation of the proletariat.

Warren Buffett Gives Wealth a Good Name

The rich in a free society are merely savers on steroids. While normal savers provide a service to society, the rich, being super-savers, provide an extraordinary service to society.

The problem of perception is that throughout history, before the emergence of the free market, during mercantilism, the rich were indeed tyrants and exploiters of the masses, either as land-holding gentry, initially earned through military service to the monarch, or as crony capitalists, with monopoly industries protected by law.

So *the instinct to suspect wealth, is natural, and was true for most of history*, but this instinct is wrong, where "liberal," non-crony markets exist.

I believe that thrift is essential to well-ordered living. - John D. Rockefeller

"Being rich is a good thing. Not just in the obvious sense of benefiting you and your family, but in the broader sense. Profits are not a zero sum game. The more you make, the more of a financial impact you can have." - Mark Cuban

"Poverty is not socialism. To be rich is glorious." - Deng Xiaoping

"I'm a millionaire; I'm a multi-millionaire. I'm filthy rich. You know why I'm a multi-millionaire? 'Cause multi-millions like what I do." - Michael Moore

"Using taxes to punish the rich, in reality, punishes everyone because we are all interconnected." - Rand Paul

SYNERGY OF CAPITAL AND LABOUR

"In a democracy, the poor will have more power than the rich because there are more of them, and the will of the majority is supreme." Aristotle

Much self-imposed poverty in the democratic world can be traced to a lack of understanding of the synergy between capital and labour, on the part of labour, in the general sense of anyone who works for a paycheck.

The wages of workers are constrained by their productivity, what the addition of their labour adds to a firm's profitability. Productivity is dependent on a firm's investment in tools, which is itself dependent on investor savings and banker lending.

Workers Require Tools to be Productive, and all Tools Represent Someone's Delayed Gratification

A worker without a tool is a worker that is not helpful to a business, more than his ability to lift and move things. **Savers who enable effort to be redirected toward capital and tools are natural allies of the workers of those tools, and vice-versa.**

The vast majority of people do not have the capacity of delayed gratification necessary to generate their own savings, investment, and equipment. They do not own, nor do they have a predisposition to own, commercial land, machinery, commercial real estate, nor large-scale electronic processing equipment.

They rather operate closer to the credo of "you only live once", which has some merit, but this value system leaves them one choice for increasing their productivity and hence wages, which is to rent capital from the saver/capitalist, directly, or indirectly through the employer/entrepreneur. This is a profitable, symbiotic relationship, an inconvenient truth *that left-leaning political activists and intellectuals find humiliating.*

"But only 'rich' people by definition have the 'extra' money to buy things and invest to create economic growth. Do we really want to tax that 'extra' money away - and give it to the government to spend? Does that make any economic sense outside of politics and our emotional desire to make everyone suffer equally through these tough times?"
- Terry Savage

"Socialism has no moral justification whatsoever; poor people are not morally superior to rich people, nor are they owed anything by rich people simply because of their lack of success." - Ben Shapiro

CAPITALISM, THE WORD

Google defines capitalism as "an economic and political system in which a country's trade and industry are controlled by private owners for profit, rather than by the state."

I think this is unhelpful in several ways. Firstly, when the average person thinks "capitalist," what comes to mind are robber barons of the trust era or *Wolf of Wall Street*, rather than someone more democratically inspiring, even "cool," like Steve Jobs of Apple, Richard Branson of Virgin, or Elon Musk of Tesla.

The link between what capitalists have contributed to society while acquiring their wealth is disconnected from the popular view of the rich. And further, "private ownership"

The Popular Perception of the Robber Baron

conjures up the mental image of one percenter inherited capital propping up their status with crony capitalism, Romney's offshore accounts, and other trickery.

The thing is, in a free society, you do have the choice of who to work for and from whom to buy products and services. Where there is an attempt at exploitation, labour simply quits and gets a job down the street. Customers move to the competition.

What is less appreciated is how much more ugly this inevitably becomes when an industry comes under the control of the government. This can occur directly or through a fiat monopoly where consumer choice is eliminated. This results in decisions being made for political purposes or bureaucratic convenience, and there is a void of the discipline and check of competition. This has to be experienced to be believed. Have you interacted with the Post Office, tax collection or vehicle licensing recently?

A better moniker for the broader implications of "Capitalism" would be "Free Market System", or coining something new, like "Marketism", which more accurately represents what it is. It is the free exchange of effort or labour, services, goods, capital equipment and real estate, money, international trade, in the open marketplace, without government coercion, which is known as Adam Smith "*Classical* Liberalism."

"Under capitalism, man exploits man. Under communism, it's just the opposite." - John Kenneth Galbraith

"Capitalism has worked very well. Anyone who wants to move to North Korea is welcome." - Bill Gates

"The problem of social organization is how to set up an arrangement under which greed will do the least harm, capitalism is that kind of a system." - Milton Friedman

ROLE OF IMPULSE CONTROL

Some of this relates to impulse control, delayed gratification, and the work done by Walter Mischel in the 1960s and 1970s at Stanford University, and its role in poverty.

Four-year-olds were given the choice between one marshmallow immediately, or two of them 15 minutes later.

When researchers followed up decades later they found that those with impulse control had higher SAT scores, better social competence and were more mature. They were better able to cope with stress, were more likely to plan ahead, were less likely to have addiction disorders, be divorced or overweight.

Impulse Control Factors Large in Socio-Economic Performance

Jed Rubenfeld and Amy Chua (infamous Tiger Mom) are Yale Law professors. Their book, *The Triple Package: How Three Unlikely Traits Explain the Rise and Fall of Cultural Groups in America* (2014) asserts that three factors explain the disproportionate success of certain cultural groups in the U.S., based on Census data and other sources.

The first factor is a sense of group superiority, such as exists in the entrepreneurial Nigerian Igbo people. The second factor is a sense of inferiority or insecurity as exists for certain individuals or sub-groups, such as immigrants, or insecurity instilled by parents. The third factor is impulse control with a capacity for delayed gratification, as suggested by the Stanford Marshmallow Experiment. Notably, all of these factors can be acquired and developed.

"Educate your children to self-control, to the habit of holding passion and prejudice and evil tendencies subject to an upright and reasoning will, and you have done much to abolish misery from their future and crimes from society." Benjamin Franklin

"Anyone can get angry, but to do this to the right person, to the right extent, at the right time, with the right motive, and in the right way, that is not for everyone, nor is it easy." Aristotle

"A miser grows rich by seeming poor. An extravagant man grows poor by seeming rich." - William Shakespeare

"Compound interest is the eighth wonder of the world. He who understands it, earns it ... he who doesn't ... pays it." - Albert Einstein

GOOD RICH DAD, BAD RICH DAD

Most people are confused between "good rich" and "bad rich". It's like when a friend's doctor said his cholesterol was high, I asked, the good type or bad type?

When we got the results for HDL and LDL, that told a different story. Rich people are like that, with "good" types and bad types. Same for poor people.

Rich people, or right-wingers, who think all the poor are lazy, are just as deluded as poor people, or left-wingers, who think all the rich are crony capitalist thieves.

Virgin's Richard Branson, Master of Creative Destruction of the Old Way of Doing Things

Some people are "economically challenged" due to choosing to be heroic immigrants; being struck by a random illness, accident or disability; uncontrollable local industry adjustments; and so on, bad luck of the draw, such that anyone other than an extremist libertarian or sadist would want to help them out.

Then there is a different category of "economically challenged" due to: lack of effort; negative attitude; disrespect of the law; those with chemical or financial addictions or low impulse control, spendaholics, gamblers; and those with a lack of appreciation for getting educated or a trade, getting and staying married, and having children after marriage.

There are very few people below the poverty line who are substance-free, educated and married, save for the genuinely unlucky of the preceding paragraph. A set of interventions designed to assist the former group would be unhelpful, even damaging if offered to the latter group, and vice versa.

A great deal of public policy does not ask the question, *good cholesterol or bad*? Same goes for rich people. One type is self-made from honest work, having created many jobs in the process and having provided quality products and services to their customers.

In a free society of aware consumers, the relationship of entrepreneur and customer represents a better deal, a more rewarding relationship than what was otherwise available. Same applies to the relationship between entrepreneur and employee; each is better off than the next available choice.

THE EVIL OF CRONY CAPITALISM

What gets some people on the wrong track is imbalanced attention to the "bad" rich, of which there are several varieties to be beware of.

Monarchy was one, where there was rule by king rather than rule by law, a problem which began to be rectified by the Magna Carta, completed when William and Mary were put on the throne by Parliament.

In the 1800s monarchs and Parliament controlled state-sponsored monopoly industries, the crony capitalist mercantilism that Adam Smith opposed.

Crony Capitalism is Mercantilism Redux

Strong man communism is monarchy by another name. World communists, monarchs, fascists and dictators, all get along very well, all being individuals or small groups telling everyone else what to do. They and their gulags are feared by the people, rather than the more progressive arrangement of the government fearing the voter.

The world is generally divided by the free and the unfree. The free have shed monarchs, mercantilists, communists, fascists, and theocrats, and the unfree are not there yet. But there is a new threat to workers and voters, the crony capitalist, or *neo-mercantilist.*

In the democratic West, this new form of "bad rich" has arisen, these firms with large lobbying budgets in the nation's capitals, buying influence. However, they cannot be blamed for pursuing their self-interest and following the rules of the game.

It is not the fault of politicians selling influence; rather it traces more to a confused and distracted electorate who is not paying attention and understanding what is going on, rewarding politicians of any stripe who play this game, and not supporting politicians, the *neo-Whigs*, the **authentic progressives,** striving for reform.

It's funding "open season" on U.S. politicians who are required to sell influence to fund campaigns. In Canada, political contributions from corporations, unions, and wealthy individuals were effectively outlawed by the radical 2003 reforms of Jean Chretien (Liberal), but Canadians still think it is normal for the government to pick winners, "invest" in green industries, and save failing companies and stressed sectors.

"Far too many well-connected businesses are feeding at the federal trough. By addressing corporate welfare as well as other forms of welfare, we would add a whole new level of understanding to the notion of entitlement reform." - Charles Koch

KOCH BROTHERS' APPLIED AUSTRIANISM

Charles Koch (born 1935) is Chairman and CEO of Koch Industries, the second-largest privately held firm in the U.S. Charles was recently ranked as 5th richest person in the U.S., along with his co-owner brother David.

They dramatically expanded the medium-sized firm inherited from his father, employing Market-Based Management, described in his 2007 book *The Science of Success.*

David & Charles Koch Translate Austrianism Into Political Action

His decentralized, dispersed-knowledge organizational approach is based on the economic theories of fellow Mont Pelerin Society members F.A. Hayek (spontaneous order) and L. Von Mises (Austrian entrepreneurial theory), as well as Israel Kirzner. He was also influenced by Adam Smith, Joseph Schumpeter, and Thomas Sowell, among others. He funded some of F.A. Hayek's research.

Charles is a libertarian (socially liberal) Republican and co-founded the Cato Institute. He is particularly opposed to crony capitalism, corporate welfare, and with his brother works with Democrats in support of criminal justice reform.

Brother David Koch (born 1940), Executive Vice-President of Koch Industries and co-owner, is the richest person in New York. In 1980, he ran for Vice-President of the U.S. on the Libertarian ticket. Dismayed by politics and some of the unrealistic positions of the Libertarian Party, he became a Republican, though he also donates to Democrats, supports the right to choose and same-sex marriage, and opposed the war on drugs and the Iraq War. He is on the board of the Cato Institute.

Charles Koch Quotes:
"Crony capitalism is much easier than competing in the open market. But it erodes our overall standard of living and stifles entrepreneurs by rewarding the politically favored rather than those who provide what consumers want."

"We all tend to pursue our own interests, but in a true market economy we can only prosper by providing others with what they value."

"I developed two strong passions. The first was to help build a great company. The second was to identify and understand the principles that lead to prosperity and societal progress. After studying history, economics, philosophy, science, psychology and other disciplines, I concluded that the two passions were strongly, indeed intimately related."

"Allowing people the freedom to pursue their own interests, within beneficial rules of just conduct, is the best and only sustainable way to promote societal progress."

ARTHUR BROOKS' MORAL ARGUMENT FOR FREE ENTERPRISE

Arthur C. Brooks (born May 21, 1964) is
president of the American Enterprise Institute
(AEI), a conservative think tank. He is an
ideological libertarian and political independent.

Brooks' path to fame was unconventional.
Following a professional decade as an orchestral
French hornist and instructor, he pressed the reset
button with a correspondence course in undergrad
in economics, following up with graduate and
Ph.D. studies in policy.

A lifelong liberal, Brooks noticed something while
helping on a campaign: Republican households
were more likely to be polite, nicer, than
Democratic households. He rose to prominence

*Brooks Composes a
Liberal Tone to
Defending Conservatism*

with his 2006 book *Who Really Cares: The Surprising Truth about Compassionate
Conservatism*, which provided evidence that conservatives give more to charity
than liberals. In his *2008 book Gross National Happiness: Why Happiness Matters
for America – and How We Can Get More of It*, he points to data that suggests that
conservatives are twice as happy as liberals.

In his 2010 book *The Battle: How the Fight between Free Enterprise and Big
Government Will Shape America's Future*, Brooks laments that while the majority
of Americans support free enterprise, the entertainment industry, and academia,
representing an influential minority, is sceptical of it. He observes that this is
feeding a culture war that is supporting ongoing momentum toward a European-
style social market economy.

In his 2012 bestseller *The Road to Freedom: How to Win the Fight for Free
Enterprise,* Brooks observes that because progressives largely base their argument
on emotional and moral arguments, this is therefore the most effective way to
defend free enterprise. The moral case includes happiness through earned success,
merit-based fairness, and ultimately, that free enterprise actually is the only
approach that has a track record of poverty reduction.

He further argues, consistent with F.A. Hayek's "progressivism," that government
should provide a limited social safety net, food, shelter, medical care, and make
interventions to market failures, when it can practically do so, without going so far
as to try to impose equality of material outcomes. Learning of Brooks' more
friendly interpretation of capitalism, the Dalai Lama in 2014 proposed to the AEI
that they conduct a two-day panel discussion on happiness and free markets. He
remarked that he had a more respect for capitalism due to the event.

CHAPTER 8 – WHAT IS SUPPLY AND DEMAND?

Teach a parrot the terms 'supply and demand' and you've got an economist.
- Thomas Carlyle

MARGINAL BOTHER (COST)

Let's say we are in the business of shovelling snow from porches. For it to be worth our while to shovel one porch, we account for the trouble of getting dressed and walking to the neighbour's porch and the cost of borrowing a shovel from a friend. We think it is worth $5 for the bother of shovelling one porch, which is what you charge.

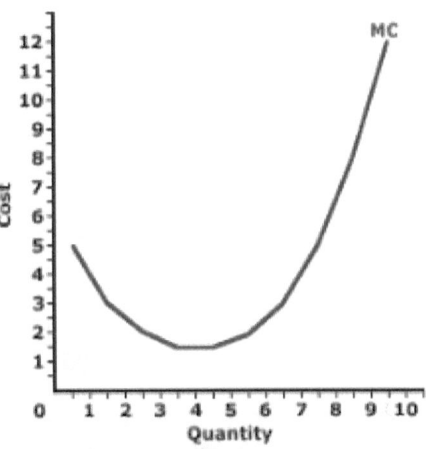

See the line to the right begin at the point of $5 cost and 1 unit of quantity. You finish the first porch and think to yourself, "I am already dressed, out here, with a shovel in hand, it would not be much bother to shovel the next neighbour's porch."

Understanding This Chart May Change Your World View

So little trouble, that you think to yourself that you could be enticed to do it for as little as $2, which corresponds to the second point of the line.

As it happens, a neighbour appears at their door waving some money and begging you to shovel the porch, and you do it for $2. After doing the second porch, you are getting momentum, warming up, and thinking, "this is easy", and you knock on a third door and offer to do it for $1.50. At $1.50 you decide that that is your bottom line, and you do the fourth porch for the same price. Next, you start to get a bit overheated and tired, and start to think about the hot chocolate you will have when you get home, so you insist on $2.00 to do the sixth porch.

With each subsequent job, you are getting more tired and fed up, wanting to call it quits for the day. You start walking home, but seeing you carrying a shovel, people are waving money, and you start insisting on higher and higher pay, to a point at which clients start shaking their heads no, which you are just fine with, and hang up the shovel for the day. This is the part of the marginal cost curve that moves steeply higher with each subsequent porch or unit.

In this simplified example, for each fatigue level, the naive shoveller only charges his best offer to each customer. This is of course not what normally happens, because in real life, the minimum price you are willing to shovel for, is not the usual way a service is priced. Rather, it is almost always priced somewhere above the lowest price you would be willing to do it for.

To delve further into how a service is priced, we are going to need a supply curve and a demand curve. Marginal cost is halfway to understanding what a supply curve is, which is discussed next.

THE SUPPLY CURVE

With all the money you made shovelling porches, your younger brother Billy, decides to get into the business.

He is shorter than you but is on the wrestling team and in great shape. He can work just as hard, with the same stamina. Now, when there is a storm, there are two guys out offering to shovel, twice the number of porches can be shovelled, for each theoretical price point of the incentive curve.

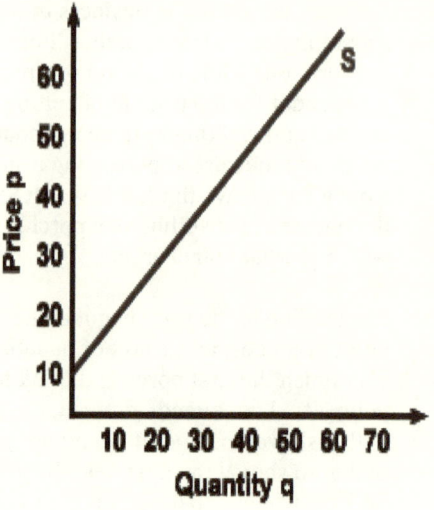

The Supply Curve, Half of the Heartbeat of the Invisible Hand

There is a monster storm, and the two guys are not keeping up. Homeowners are offering $30, even $40 to shovel a porch. At these prices, the entire football team hears about it and gets motivated, and they are collectively clearing 30, even 40 porches at these price levels, each working as independent shovellers, walking around with shovels, looking for clients.

The supply curve is the lateral addition of each shoveller's marginal cost curve. It's not something invented by economists, it is rather a natural phenomena of reality, observed and described, in this case, described in a graph, which is a metaphor for something real. In this example, no one is shovelling at $9, and at $60, there is enough incentive to get 70 porches shovelled, on aggregate.

Hopefully, you are starting to see the importance of the supply curve and its meaning. It is a summation of an entire industry collectively, what effort that industry is willing to provide for each price point regarding a number of units of sales or service, which flows from the marginal bother, the marginal cost, of each additional unit.

For a firm, the marginal bother is not getting tired and hot, nor the cost of renting the shovel from a neighbour, it is rather all the marginal, or additional, financial costs to the firm of producing each additional unit. This is separate to the fixed start-up costs, and is also different than the average cost per unit.

Fixed cost is the money spent before producing the first unit for the shoveller, the bother of getting dressed and going out, the cost of the shovel rental. Once he is out and knocking on doors, the cost is then the time away from playing video games, fatigue, discomfort.

But this is only half of the market story. So what is a demand curve?

The Market Demand Curve, the Supply Curve's "Better Half."

For the marginal cost curves, we described the price at which each individual shoveller was willing to provide so many units of porch shovelling, or alternatively, the number of porches they were willing to shovel for each price point. We explained how the supply curve was the lateral addition of all the individual marginal cost curves. This is a lot of market information summarized in one line.

Similarly, the demand curve is a lateral addition of each individual porch owner's demand curve. Let's look at Consumer 1. At a price of $1, he is taking five units of porch shovelling, he is getting his porch shovelled, he is getting his back step shovelled, the driveway, and he is looking at the roof of the garage.

At $6 he is shovelling his own porch or waiting for spring, and at $5 he is just getting the porch done. His neighbour has the same demand curve. When you add the two together laterally, you get the market demand curve. This curve represents the preferences and behaviour of all of the porch owners collectively. Again, a lot of information contained in one line.

To repeat, this is a representational metaphor for something that exists in reality, perceived or not, understood or not, measured or not. It is half of the heartbeat of the invisible hand.

We now see how supply responds to price, and how demand responds to price, but how do we establish the price and quantity that a market will settle on? Next are supply and demand together.

"Rock star preaches capitalism—wow. Sometimes I hear myself and I just cannot believe it. But commerce is real, that's what you're about here. It's real. Aid is just a stop-gap. Commerce, entrepreneurial capitalism takes more people out of poverty than aid -- of course, we know that." - Bono

SUPPLY & DEMAND

When you overlay a demand curve on a supply curve, there is only one place where they intersect, which is called equilibrium.

It is the only combination of price and quantity at which shovellers and porch owners are in agreement. At prices higher, demand is less than the quantity supplied. At prices lower, supply is less than the quantity demanded.

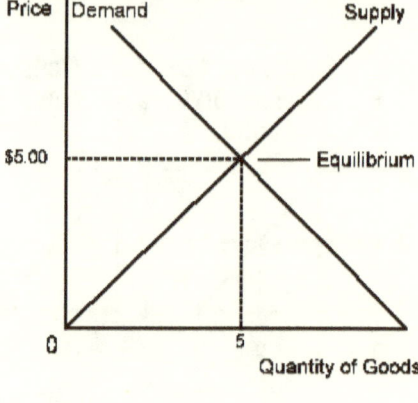

Excess supply provides an incentive for the shovellers to lower price to stay busy and earning. Excess demand incents the porch owners to raise the price to attract shovellers. An excess of any kind

Supply & Demand Together Locates the Sweet Spot for Consumers and Producers

naturally incents adjustment of price toward equilibrium, without anyone being aware of or understanding this underlying, invisible process.

While the supply curve summarizes the preferences and behaviour of shovellers, and the demand curve summarizes the preferences and behaviour of porch owners, the two lines together represent the entire marketplace and the interaction between the two. A lot of information. Any gathering of suppliers and demanders of a service or product will *spontaneously* order itself along these self-stabilizing lines, unless someone, or something, interferes with the "free" market.

A government might choose to impose a price cap, but this would lead to a condition of excess demand as players are not permitted to raise prices to organically ration supply. In a state of excess demand, allocation is done by a means other than price, such as rationing, lines, first-come-first-serve, special shops for the politically connected, and so on.

Or, a large company might buy up all the small companies and become a monopolist. Under this scenario, the monopolist sees an opportunity to artificially restrict supply and raise prices, moving up the demand curve which unnaturally increases profits.

Most of what economists complain about are interferences in the market by governments or failures of the market, such as the emergence of a monopolist, which lead to price and quantity being pushed away from the point of equilibrium, that single combination of price and quantity at which suppliers and demanders agree.

Supply and demand can relate to snow shovelling, which is a service, shovels, which is a product, jobs at Macdonald's, which is labour, mortgages, which is capital.

THE SUPPLY VERSUS DEMAND ECONOMY

The path of history is largely represented by the life-cycle of birthing, shifting, and destructing of demand curves. For example, there arises a generic demand for information management, starting with oral traditions, papyrus, printing and then the digital age.

Supply curves normally arise in response to demand curves, eventually shaped and positioned according to the organic cost of producing and supplying the product or service at each production quantity, including a factor for entrepreneurial and worker taste for providing the service.

Each person plays a split-personality role in the demand and supply sides of the economy, wearing two hats. As long as each individual and society as a whole lets demand lead, and supply follow, civilization progresses as rapidly as possible through innovation and creative destruction to the next economic plateau, which inevitably raises all boats.

Every Person Wears Two Hats, as a Consumer and a Worker.

At all times, there is the temptation of supply to reverse this relationship by attempting to coerce demand. This is done through the many expressions of crony capitalism to leverage state power to pick winners, unfair trade practices to create an oligopoly or monopoly, or unionization for the purpose of coercing wages beyond the spontaneous market level reflective of the contribution of each worker to the bottom line.

In the extreme case of the state monopoly, the relationship between supply and demand is reversed from its natural order. Consumers serve at the pleasure and convenience of the entity and its unionized workers. The entity and its workers are vested in the status quo, innovation is the enemy, and creative destruction is replaced by uncreative preservation. It is incented to do less for higher prices, pulling back along the supply curve toward the monopolists' optimum of providing less for higher prices.

In the more organic demand-driven economy, all specific supply curves serve at the pleasure of the consumer: the firms, their capital investors, their entrepreneurs, their executives, but as well their workers. Without the protection of the overwhelming force of a monopoly such as the Standard Oil Trust or protection through government fiat such as regulations that limit market entry, *conditions are optimal when the status quo is naked in the face of a better, more efficient way of doing things*.

So Dell and Apple slay the IBM PC. Yahoo slays Altavista, and Google slays Yahoo. Droid and Google Project Fi challenge Apple. What would the world look like if we collectively decided that all those IBM mainframe jobs needed to be protected in the 1980s?

YOU'VE BEEN UBERED

To Uber, or not to Uber, that is the question. Uber is a verb which refers to the act of riding Uber, as directed. There is also "to be Ubered", which has come to mean your job or industry has just been "creatively destructed", disturbed, or severely stressed by the invisible fist, in the form of a new sharing-economy app such Uber.

In the past, freelance cabs arose as a supply response to the demand (curve) to simply get around by those who did not have carriages or cars. In response to a few bad apples, cities began to register and license cabs for the protection of consumers, however, regulation creates a mechanism by which supply can coerce demand. Supply always seeks to coerce demand.

Travis Kalanick, Uber CEO

In most cities the cab industry used the carrot of political contributions and the stick of civil disobedience and striking to coerce city councils to flip consumer regulation into rather protecting the cab industry itself from competition and consumers. They understandably followed the incentive crumbs in the forest, acting like a monopolist, raising prices and lobbying for the restriction of new licenses. With growing populations and lack of a commensurate increase in drivers, they restricted the spontaneous growth of the supply curve and rather moved up the demand curve to higher prices and unnatural and distortive profits.

Then they go a step further. This somewhat pedestrian level of market corruption is leveraged into a true economic abomination. City councils permitted these licenses to be traded in the open market, enabling a few families to buy up and control most of a city's taxi plates. Finally, they channeled some of this crony capitalist wealth into support for pro-taxi politicians during election campaigns. The unnatural profits translated into higher taxi plate prices. Capital gains flowed to the handful of individuals who own the plates. The drivers themselves arbitraged their income to the natural level by tolerating excessive plate rental fees.

Into this mess steps Uber who creates a bylaw-smashing end run around the scam by given city councils plausible deniability during efforts to stamp Uber out. This ends up being a litmus test for the market "progressiveness" of each city government. It created an opportunity for ethical councils to unwind the mess given that Uber was doing the dirty job of creatively destructing the abomination for them.

Councils, still firmly in the hands of the taxi unions or the local union consortium, made a more sincere effort to chase Uber out of town, missing the opportunity to be on the right side of history. So now we have two distinct types of towns.

CHAPTER 9 - FAILURE OF GOVERNMENT

Every decent man is ashamed of the government he lives under. - H. L. Mencken

BANKRUPTING THE KIDS

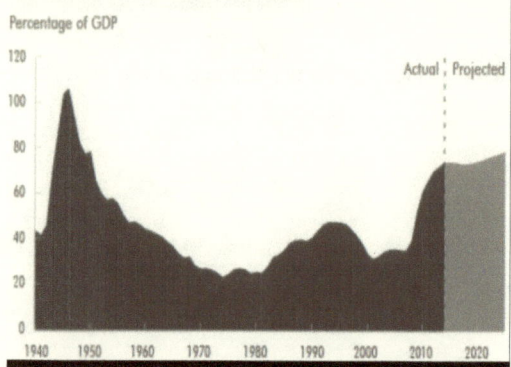

Federal Debt Held by the Public

Percentage of GDP

Actual ¦ Projected

1940 1950 1960 1970 1980 1990 2000 2010 2020

U. S.

This points to a key issue: what is kindness, and who is being kind on each side of the budget argument. It boils down to a question of sustainability.

When a retirement planner admonishes a client for not saving enough, is he being unkind?

When a tiger mom browbeats a teenager into doing their homework or going to college, is she being unkind? Certainly not, and I think anyone who would be confused by this, is living emotionally, with a very limited horizon of first-round effects, rather than rationally, with a long-term horizon, an awareness of second and third-round effects.

Why are modern "progressives" so hyper-attuned to environmental sustainability, but so blind to financial sustainability? Is it possible that behind: ineffective; feel-good, activist environmentalism; making the rich pay with higher taxes in real time; and, borrowing against the future, is a "socialism lite", and behind socialism is resentment of, and revenge against the rich, by impulsive "marshmallow eaters" on a grand scale?

"If I owe you a pound, I have a problem; but if I owe you a million, the problem is yours." -John Maynard Keynes

"Rather go to bed supperless, than rise in debt." -Benjamin Franklin

"Blessed are the young for they shall inherit the national debt." - Herbert Hoover

"The principle of spending money to be paid by posterity, under the name of funding, is but swindling futurity on a large scale." - Thomas Jefferson

"He who will not economize will have to agonize." - Confucius

"Government spending is taxation. When you look at this, I've never heard of a poor person spending himself into prosperity; let alone I've never heard of a poor person taxing himself into prosperity." - Arthur Laffer

"A liberal is someone who feels a great debt to his fellow man; a debt he proposes to pay off with your money." -Gordon Liddy

THE POVERTY TRAP

Unemployment support for those without a job, through no fault of their own, a worthy thing, starts to be baked into the economic cake of multigenerational, seasonal employment, by intention.

Existing industries symbiotically adapt with hiring and layoff practises adjusted to harmonize with seasonal financial assistance. Yes, companies are subject to incentives and moral hazard!

Work *for the* Dole

An Australian Government Initiative

Socialistic Countries are Learning That They Can No Longer Pay Citizens to Stay at Home

Even entire industries are established from conception to exploit programs as a third round effect, building a flow of wealth from productive geographies to unproductive geographies and disincenting internal domestic migration. Sadly, this is the opposite of what successful societies, individuals, and families do, who rather move toward where the work and opportunity are.

Rather than pay people to stay in low employment geographies, a better, more rational program would incent migration toward jobs.

Welfare, unthoughtfully constructed or administered, as was the case before the Clinton reforms, can incent having children outside of marriage, and divorce, primary vectors of poverty.

Human psychology, at the individual level, and the economy at the macro level, begins to adjust to such incentives, like a developing teenage body adjusting to and getting addicted to nicotine. Multi-generational families, as subject to moral hazard as anyone, adapt to exploiting welfare and support programs. Assistance ineffectively supervised can be blended with off-books cash income.

Caring societies, like caring parents, do not permit an able individual or family to get comfortable on social assistance, no more than a caring family would permit a healthy, able, college grad to get comfortable living at home and not moving forward with their lives.

"You cannot help men permanently by doing for them what they could and should do for themselves." - Abraham Lincoln

"The urge to save humanity is almost always a false front for the urge to rule." H. L. Mencken

65

THE CONFLICT OF INTEREST TRAP

"It is difficult to get a man to understand something when his job depends on not understanding it" - Upton Sinclair

Social support programs, in conception, defendable programs, in practice can become a target for manipulation and outright fraud. Unsupervised and out of sight to taxpayers, following the principle of "other people's money," they evolve into cash cows for the administering bureaucrats as much as for the target client group.

This applies to all government programs. Politicians, administrators, and regulators are as equally subject to moral hazard as anyone else. As a general rule, politicians rely on government administrators for policy advice on the programs they manage, programs that these same administrators are dependent on for their careers.

Effective governments take care to mitigate moral hazard and conflict of interest on the part of administering and regulating bureaucracies.

Upon creating a program with a budget, one also creates various helper groups with a vested interest in the health or cash flow of the program. Most of the time, the power, and influence of these vested helper groups exceeds the power and self-interest of the target helpee group. It always exceeds the focus and concentration of interest of the average taxpayer, such that, programs that actually damage the target group are kept on life support or even doubled-down on, as key players follow their incentives.

Effective market progressive governments act reluctantly to create new programs, understanding the challenges and likely harm of most governmental interventions.

"Any change is resisted because bureaucrats have a vested interest in the chaos in which they exist." - Richard Nixon

"Every time you cut programs, you take away a person who has a vested interest in high taxes, and you put him on the tax rolls and make him a taxpayer" - Grover Norquist

"Every election is a sort of advance auction sale of stolen goods." - H. L. Mencken

"Government should enforce rule of law. It should enforce contracts, it should protect people bodily from being attacked by criminals. And when the government does those things, it is facilitating liberty. When it goes beyond those things, it becomes destructive to both human happiness and human liberty." - Grover Norquist

GREAT INTENTIONS, TERRIBLE RESULTS

"One of the great mistakes is to judge policies and programs by their intentions rather than their results." Milton Friedman

Politicians who don't believe in economics, or lack business experience, often begin with an intention, and there it ends.

Any feel-good, shoot from the hip program, divorced from science, measurement and results, will do.

This group wraps itself in the flag of compassion, and condemns the empiricists as cold-hearted, even haters.

But in the end, it is naive, well-intentioned, but ineffective policy, which harms. Like the softhearted co-dependent sister who keeps sending money to the addicted brother who rather needs rehab. Feels good, but is not actually helping.

So capitalism is not actually about the capitalists and the one percent, it's about the power of markets, and freedom from governmental distortions, to craft the best overall result for individuals of any lifestyle or socioeconomic class.

It's about crafting solutions that firstly, do no harm, and we know much does do harm, but following, uses economic reality, incentives, to empower and motivate the individual worker or business start-up entrepreneur, to leverage this force which happily already exists in reality, in the absence of government interference.

Same as the human body, which knows how to heal itself, if it is allowed to heal itself. Much of this is laissez-faire, simply getting out of the way.

Where there is market failure, like needing to raise an army for national defence, or feeding the homeless, the guiding principle is to achieve the objective while minimizing interference and distortion of incentives, the core engine of efficiency, effectiveness and societal wealth, the ultimate determinant of the size of the economic pie which pays for social programming.

"Hell is full of good wishes or desires" - Saint Bernard of Clairvaux (c. 1150)

"Spending is not caring. Spending is what politicians do instead of caring. Spending more does not guarantee success. Politicians like to measure spending because it is easier than measuring actual metrics of accomplishment." – Grover Norquist

BUREAUCRATS GONE WILD!

"Moral Hazard: Lack of incentive to guard against risk when one is protected from its consequences." - Wikipedia

The problem here is an inconvenient truth, the phenomena of moral hazard.

The term was borrowed from the insurance industry where it was

used to refer to the moral hazard of torching your business for the insurance money. It was tweaked by economics in the sixties to mean an inefficient appreciation for risk.

Helping people in a predictable way creates an incentive for the helpee to exploit the helper and for them to take on more risk than they would spontaneously. Reforms that start out as good and necessary things such as unionization, unemployment support, welfare, and social security disability, can pass the point of economic and social helpfulness and overshoot into diminishing returns, harming society overall.

"Government does not solve problems; it subsidizes them." Ronald Reagan

Government employees, being human beings who respond to incentives, who are not saints, become part of the moral hazard equation, eventually existing in codependency with the program helpee client.

The half of the economy that is taxed and spent by politicians, bureaucrats, school boards, fire departments, the military and so on, by design, lacks 1) the self-regulating discipline of competition, 2) the discipline of having to face a consumer, and 3) the discipline of facing an arms-length government regulator.

Nevertheless, regulators themselves are subject to moral hazard and the tendency to go native, acquiring the relationship status of a colleague to those he or she regulates, or worse, becoming part of a revolving door between the regulated and the regulators.

Staff of the Minerals Management Service (MMS), the agency responsible for regulating the Deepwater Horizon, who's failed drilling rig spilled millions of gallons of crude into the Gulf, upon investigation, were found to have had sexual relationships with energy company representatives. They accepted gifts, meals, sporting event tickets and free holidays from the firms they were overseeing. It is reported that the energy companies would write the regulator reports in pencil for them, and MMS staff would copy them over in ink.

"Governments are not representative. They have their own power, serving segments of the population that are dominant and rich." - Noam Chomsky

FAILURE OF GOVERNMENT

In truth, an organic economy is a gift of nature that knows how to heal itself, as long as we let nature take its course. We should only intervene under very limited circumstances where we see what is termed, "market failure."

Like holistic medicine, one must intervene sparingly, minimally, with humility and great respect for the likelihood of doing more harm than good. Economics, *as it is currently practised by politicians*, is like 19th Century medicine, using leeches and blood-letting as medical treatment.

Market Failure: "scenarios where individuals' pursuit of pure self-interest leads to results that are not efficient, that can be improved upon from the societal point of view" – Wikipedia.

Examples include inefficiency and exploitation of the citizenry due to: natural monopoly; public lack of information; pollution; or overuse of public property. While there is great attention to market failure, there is less attention to g*overnment failure,* also known as *non-market failure*, where the medicine is worse than the illness.

Government failure occurs when government intervenes too little (i.e. the Federal Reserve during the depression), too much (i.e. British nationalization of transportation and energy sectors), or ineffectively (i.e. regulation of Gulf of Mexico oil wells).

The term "government failure" was coined by British Nobel economist Ronald Coase in 1964 when he drew attention to economists' unipolar attention to market failure, with no attention to how government may cause worse problems than the original challenge.

"The truth is in California you can't build a new manufacturing facility, and businesses are leaving in droves because of bad government policy." - Carly Fiorina

"I would like to say to Milton and Anna (Friedman): Regarding the Great Depression, you're right. We did it. We're very sorry." - Ben Bernanke (Federal Reserve Chair)

"If a politician found he had cannibals among his constituents, he would promise them missionaries for dinner." - H. L. Mencken

GROVER NORQUIST – POLITICAL AUSTRIANIST

Grover Norquist, born in 1956 the son of a vice president of Polaroid Corporation, volunteered on his first national campaign at age 12. He has an M.B.A. from Harvard.

He started his career as executive director of the National Taxpayers Union and then was Economist and Chief Speechwriter for the U.S. Chamber of Commerce. He co-authored Newt Gingrich's 1994 Contract with America before founding Americans for Tax Reform (ATR) in 1985, apparently at the urging of Ronald Reagan.

ATR's goal is to reduce government revenue as a percentage of GDP. His *Wednesday Meeting Series* is a clearinghouse for the conservative movement. Norquist himself is a libertarian-leaning Republican. He supports comprehensive immigration reform, lower defense spending, and dramatically higher

Norquist's Conservative War on Big Government

levels of immigration. He is on the advisory board of LGBT conservative GOProud. He is married to a Palestinian Muslim.

He is most known for his *Taxpayer Protection Pledge* to block any increases in marginal tax rates. It has been signed by virtually all congressional Republicans. In 2011, Harry Reid claimed that Republicans "are being led like puppets by Grover Norquist." The Wall Street Journal reported that Norquist was "the Grand Central Station" of conservatism.

Grover Norquist Quotes:
"I'm not in favor of abolishing the government. I just want to shrink it down to the size where we can drown it in the bathtub."

"The Democratic Party is made up of trial lawyers, labor unions, government employees, big city political machines, the coercive utopians, the radical environmentalists, feminists, and others who want to restructure society with tax dollars and government fiat."

"What Mae West said about sex is true about taxes. All tax cuts are good tax cuts; even bad tax cuts are good tax cuts."

"I think it's very important to always make sure that you're talking to the entire coalition and to as many Americans as possible; not to go chasing after one little group or another. "

THE SOCIAL INDUSTRIAL COMPLEX

"The welfare state is not really about the welfare of the masses. It's about the egos of the elites." - Thomas Sowell

Sadly, a great deal of the social industrial complex is tainted, not only by naive do-gooders with sincere but misguided intentions, but it is as well tainted by Machiavellian "rent seeking" actors (EconoSpeak for "people rationally acting for their own interests, selfishly and effectively).

Many look to dupe the naive by pandering for political currency or exploiting the unfortunate for personal financial or career gain. *A department of welfare, acting rationally, rent seeking, no more seeks to eliminate welfare clients than a dentist wishes to eliminate cavities.*

Let's not be naive regarding the motivations and intentions of the social industrial complex. While your average welfare officer may have empathy for the poor, your average senior welfare bureaucrat may be completely detached from the human element. They have accumulated a lifetime of personal sacrifices to climb to the top, they are principally motivated to maintain the health of their institution and career, and largely move up the organization filtered on this basis.

They were preceded by leaders with the same motivation, who themselves selected future leaders on the basis of this characteristic, following this institutional Darwinian paradigm. Organizations that do not acquire this adaptive characteristic are not still here. Public institutions, while initially created for the common good, become themselves organisms subject to the Darwinian principle of survival of the fittest.

All this would be well and good, except, it ends up diminishing the size of the economic pie that is available to slice up, even directly damaging those a policy wishes to help. An economy is like a growing child, but if you feed the child empty calories and load them up with drugs, boost them with caffeine in the morning, tamp them down with alcohol at night, you are not going to end up with a productive, healthy adult, at the end of the day. *As with a natural diet's impact on the body, prosperity is created through smartly regulated, fair, free exchange between capital, entrepreneurs, employees and customers.*

"I think the best way of doing good to the poor, is not making them easy in poverty, but leading or driving them out of it. In my youth, I travelled much, and I observed in different countries, that the more public provisions were made for the poor, the less they provided for themselves, and of course became poorer. And, on the contrary, the less was done for them, the more they did for themselves, and became richer."
— Benjamin Franklin, 1766

THOMAS SOWELL ON THE SOCIAL INDUSTRIAL COMPLEX

Thomas Sowell's father died while he was in his mother's womb. His housemaid mother could not afford the children she already had, so he was adopted by his great-aunt. He was a gifted student, the first of his family to attend high school, but dropped out due to lack of money.

Sowell's War on Utopian Statist Elitism

Years following, he did exceptionally well on some university night courses. His professors got him into Harvard. He followed up with a masters from Columbia and a Ph.D. from Chicago in economics.

While working in Washington he observed and raised the alarm, on the damage done by the minimum wages that his office managed. He was shocked that his managers cared more for their own jobs than helping the poor, triggering his neoconservative flip from Marxism.

He is currently a Senior Fellow of the pro-free-enterprise Hoover Institution, holding the Rose and Milton Friedman Senior Fellowship. What Bjorn Lomborg is to environmentalism, Sowell is to the economics of welfare, race, multiculturalism, affirmative action, minimum wages, and the war on drugs.

In his 1987 book, *A Conflict of Visions*, he explains that the great political divide is based on two visions. One, a flawed utopian belief that mankind is good and that there exists an elite that can be trusted to run things for the benefit of others, without constraint. Or two, a more realistic belief that mankind largely acts out of self-interest, including its intellectual elites, and that society must be structured around this inconvenient truth, with constraints.

Sample Sowel Quotations:
"If you have always believed that everyone should play by the same rules and be judged by the same standards, that would have gotten you labeled a radical 60 years ago, a liberal 30 years ago and a racist today."

"What multiculturalism boils down to is that you can praise any culture in the world except Western culture, and you cannot blame any culture in the world except Western culture."

"The biggest and most deadly 'tax' rate on the poor comes from a loss of various welfare state benefits - food stamps, housing subsidies and the like - if their income goes up."

"Helping those who have been struck by unforeseeable misfortunes is fundamentally different from making dependency a way of life."

CHAPTER 10 - SOCIALISM

"The more people who are dependent on government handouts, the more votes the left can depend on for an ever-expanding welfare state." - Thomas Sowell

"There is all the difference in the world between treating people equally and attempting to make them equal" - F.A. Hayek

"Conservatives divide the world in terms of good and evil while liberals do it in terms of the rich and poor." - Dennis Prager

COMMUNIST PILGRIMS

Radical Puritans, called English Separatists, believed that the Church of England was beyond reform. They separated themselves and met illegally.

In 1609, they fled England to work in the textile mills of the more religiously tolerant Leiden, Holland. However, the English persecutions followed them to Holland, having angered the Crown with publications that circulated back to England.

The Pilgrims Started

Out As Communists

In 1620, they set sail for America via England. The London merchants who were financing the adventure had a strange condition, which was that all production be done communally and owned in common, with the participants entering indentured service for seven years.

After payment to the investors, the proceeds were to be equally divided among the colonists. Sadly, this provided no incentive to work, with even the most industrious becoming discouraged by the injustice of the freeloaders. The crop was so disastrous that half the colony starved to death in the first winter.

Governor Bradford wrote about the experience:

"For this community was found to breed much confusion and discontent, and retard much employment that would have been to their benefit and comfort. For young men that were most able and fit for labour and service did repine that they should spend their time and strength to work for others men's wives and children without recompense ... that was thought injustice."

They reversed course and instituted private property rights and the right to profit from their own efforts, on the basis of the family unit. Young persons without families were attached to a family unit for the purposes of production.

Bradford subsequently wrote: "This had very good success for it made all hands industrious, so as much more corn was planted than otherwise would have been."

Many of the colony who had begged off working on the corn or washing, suddenly became energetic once they realized they would starve or live in dirty clothing unless they did it for themselves.

"That which is common to the greatest number has the least care bestowed upon it." Aristotle

KARL MARX ON SOCIALISM AND COMMUNISM

Hunter-gatherer societies practised "primitive communism", which produced limited capital (tools and structures) and consequently, a subsistence living.

The Communist Manifesto was published by Karl Marx in 1848. He observed that as the lords revolted against the king with the Magna Carta, the merchants overthrew the mercantilist lords, leading to capitalism. He asserted that the workers would revolt against the capitalists, firstly to form socialism, which is public ownership of enterprise, and then secondly to form communism, which is the elimination of all private property and differences in income.

When Marx Wrote Das Kapital, There Was No Theory of the Entrepreneur and Creative Destruction

"Communism" the word derives from the Latin *communis*, meaning common or universal. "Socialism" derives from the Latin *sociare*, meaning to combine or share, attributed to French economist Pierre-Henri Leroux (1797-1871) from his work "*Individualism and Socialism.*" At conception, he himself warned of the limitations of extreme applications of individualism or socialism.

Marxism flows from a presumption that an economy is a static store of wealth, that can simply be sliced up without consequences. It ignores where wealth comes from, suggesting that the workers through revolution might profit from seizing the means of production, without understanding the type of individual who creates said means of production. People do not question just how all that stuff actually gets invented, developed, made and shipped to the Costco warehouse.

While Russia and China learned the disastrous results of communism by actually implementing it, America avoided this, in no small part due to an enlightened labour movement. After flirting with socialism, American Federation of Labour President Samuel Gompers rejected the influence of the intellectuals and socialists in the labour movement. He said "Socialism holds nothing but unhappiness for the human race" and "Socialism is the fad of fanatics ... and it has no place in the hearts of those who would secure the fight for freedom and preserve democracy."

German Kaiser Wilhelm I sustained radical attacks and feared a duplication of the socialist Paris Commune of 1871 in Germany. Otto Von Bismarck staved off socialism in the 1880s by suppressing it politically while at the same time introducing the welfare state, somewhat as conceived by Marx and Engels, to quell unrest. Programs included accident, health and disability insurance as well as retirement pensions, a half century before similar programs were introduced by Labour in Britain, and 120 years before the Affordable Care Act (Obamacare) was instituted in the U.S.

"Democracy is the road to socialism. Socialism leads to communism." - Karl Marx

The Whigs opposed the Anglican monopoly and the absolute power of the monarch. They were reformers, counterbalancing the Tory Party.

This spirit of reform naturally bled into support for free trade and free markets. This was in opposition to state sponsored mercantilism, tariffs, and monopolies. It was the launching point of early liberalism, now referred to as *classical* liberalism.

Neoclassical liberalism in the late 19th century was the view that individual economic liberty depended on *minimization of government*. In the extreme, it was socially Darwinistic, similar to *right-libertarianism* of the current era.

Economic liberalism is centred on the efficiency of individual decision-making in the economy. It supports freedom of labour and private capital movement, free trade, and minimal public interference in economic decisions, other than to deconstruct private monopolies and provide public goods (not provided by the private sector). It opposes feudalism, mercantilism, socialism, market socialism and central-planning.

Social liberalism, like modern liberalism, focusses on social justice issues such as employment and income inequality, health insurance, education and training, and civil rights.

The term "*neoliberalism*" of the 1930s, also known as the "*social market economy*," represented an attempt to compromise between the weaknesses of *classical* (economic) liberalism, incorrectly blamed for the depression, without going so far as central-planning.

"*Modern* (American) liberalism" spans social liberalism in combination with the social market economy.

The term neoliberalism, currently employed as an insult from the left, was much later revived, initially in Spanish in the 1970s. This was in response to Chile's (successful) assault on the social market economy with Chicago School reforms. Tariffs, taxes, inflation and state ownership of the means of production were rolled back.

Through and beyond the New Deal, with a nudge from John Maynard Keynes and socialist economists, it can be argued that modern liberalism has drifted into representing policies that vastly surpass necessary market failure corrections and rational public works approaches to unemployment. Social liberalism has morphed into identity politics and victimology. The social market economy has been refocussed on income inequality and shifted to *Robin Hood* liberalism.

JOHN LOCKE, FATHER OF LIBERALISM

Locke's lawyer Puritan father was an English Civil War cavalry captain fighting against the King.

Locke became a doctor, eventually becoming the personal physician of Lord Anthony Ashley Cooper, the first Earl of Shaftesbury, a founder of the Whigs.

Being credited with saving Shaftesbsury's life, he was rewarded with various commercial trade-related posts, including regulation of the slave trade, which shaped his later writing.

In his dangerously revolutionary *Two Treatises of* Government (1689), anonymously published and never acknowledged during his lifetime, he attacked the biblical arguments for the divine right of kings, it being a form of slavery, the latter being equivalently immoral and in violation of natural rights.

Because persons own themselves, they by logic own their labour and the property that arises from their labour, hence the immorality of property confiscation by the state. This view was attacked by Marxists as justifying capitalism.

Further, he describes a "social contract" whereby citizens submit to the authority of an *elected* government in exchange for the protection of their natural rights, primarily protection of family and property from violence and war. There also exists the right to revolution against an illegitimate government.

In his three *Letter[s] Concerning Toleration (1689-1692)* he presented the argument for religious tolerance and separation of church and state.

Suspected of involvement in a plot to assassinate the king, he fled to the Netherlands in 1683. He returned with Princess Mary to join with King William of Orange following the establishment of Constitutional monarchy at the time of the Glorious Revolution. At this time, he became the intellectual leader of the Whigs. His writings came to prominence on both sides of the Atlantic leading up to the American Revolution.

Locke Quotes:

"All wealth is the product of labor."

"New opinions are always suspected, and usually opposed, without any other reason but because they are not already common."

"The discipline of desire is the background of character."

THE SOCIAL MARKET ECONOMY

The 1930s interwar German Freiburg School of economic thought was a descendant of the Prussian Historical School. It promoted ordoliberalism, named after the acronym of a related academic journal.

This was a low tax, pro-competition theory. Rejecting Marxism but not going so far as neoliberalism, it held the belief

The German Social Market Economy Is Very Austrian

that industry requires the firm hand of government to maintain order, in particular, to protect citizens from monopolies and crony capitalism.

Further, government should not overreach to the point of Keynesianistic steering, let alone socialist acquisition of industry, as is the case with command-control communism, *market* socialism (government ownership of the means of production in a market framework) or *democratic* socialism (government ownership of the means of production but under democratic governance).

Separately, the government is at the same time charged with maintaining a robust, personal social welfare system. These two objectives formed the basis of the post-WW II *social market economy*, "a third way" between collectivism and market liberalism. Under the "German Miracle", GDP doubled in 10 years due to the removal of wage and price controls and rationing, and the lowering marginal tax rates from 85% to 18%.

While the reboot of the German economy is popularly attributed to Marshall Plan aid from the U.S., the reality was that this assistance was on par with the level of wartime reparations payments flowing back to the allies, netting to an insignificant overall stimulus to the German economy. Also, Marshall Plan expenditures were more focused on industrial allies such as Britain and France.

Related, Nordic Social Democracy (a.k.a. Nordic Model, Nordic Capitalism) began as an evolutionary path to socialism. Following relatively minimal military engagement in the world wars and the Marshall Plan, Nordic countries course-corrected to pro-capitalist, albeit cooperative pro-unionism. They retained private ownership of all but basic public utilities, while at the same time rejecting crony capitalism and corporate welfare.

A flat income tax incented work. Employer absolute hiring and firing flexibility, in combination with a robust public safety net, allowed firms to shed workers under the creative destruction principle. The government guaranteed health care, childcare, pensions and generous social support during such transitions, freeing firms from the distraction of social policy objectives.

TOUGH LOVE - SOFT HATE

"Tough love" was coined by Bill Milliken in his book of that name in 1968. The core of tough love is this issue of the human response to incentives and moral hazard.

It is "tough" because it has an appearance of heartlessness, at first glance. For example, the parents who force a child into rehab. The coach who demands a high standard of performance. Notwithstanding this, substantive abuse may wrap itself in the banner of tough love, but this does not negate the validity of the concept.

Soft Hate, the Mirror Image of Tough Love

It's like that Subaru TV commercial where you see what is presumably a father standing and watching a teenage girl change a tire. There is an initial impression that the fellow is a lazy jerk. The denouement of the drama is that this is dad teaching daughter to be *safe-through-independence*, as opposed to being *unsafe-through-co-dependence*.

As a society, we must guard against governmental interventions that teach people to be unsafe-through-co-dependence.

"Codependent relationships are a type of dysfunctional helping relationship where one person supports or enables another person's addiction, poor mental health, immaturity, irresponsibility, or under-achievement." - Wikipedia

In this story is the core concept of good public policy: where individuals do not have a dad, mom, grandparent, sibling, teaching them to be safe through personal independence, governments should try best they can to fulfil that role. This proves harder than it looks, because, politicians, bureaucrats, regulators, lobbyists, are themselves human, and subject to personal incentives and the corruption of moral hazard, with no filial (family, kinship connection) motivation to actually be helpful, effectively loving, toward the less fortunate.

Governments should strive to be more like effective families when dealing with people who are economically frustrated.

While tough love looks like heartlessness on the surface, it is *effective* caring in the end. The reality is that the good but ultimately unhelpful *intentions* of many family and governmental interventions are the opposite. It looks like caring on the surface but is ineffective, co-dependent or even harmful in the end. This is worthy of the moniker, *"soft hatred"*, the mirror image of *tough love*.

FRIEDMAN'S NEGATIVE INCOME TAX

Economic science looks at minimum wages and proposes a better way. It rather suggests letting market prices find their natural level so that the market clears at zero unemployment. The progressive part is that if you don't like the wage the market settles on, you subsidize it through the tax system.

Milton Friedman popularized the idea of the negative income tax, first proposed by British politician, Liberal Juliet Evangeline (1898–1964) in the 1940s. Earned income tax credits are a form of negative income tax, but with an implicit work component. For example, let's say we assume a minimum living wage of $15 per hour.

Friedman's Market Solution to Poverty

If an employer is willing to pay someone with no skills, just out of prison, $1 per hour, the state steps in and makes up the difference, kicking in $14 per hour. This is in place of unemployment insurance, welfare, and food stamps, not only saving the transfer payments but as well saving the administrative overhead of these complex programs.

Taken one step further, if the market values their work below $1 per hour, the state could provide workfare and/or training. Alternatively, the state could pay the person $15 per hour, and as well as subsidize the job creator, whatever it takes to put the person in a job, as *effective* compassion, rather than disability insurance or welfare.

The idea is that that person will acquire skills to eventually become independent, failing that, it will mitigate the risk of not drifting into deeper trouble, requiring expensive intervention by police, health care, or the corrections system.

A negative employment-based income, or even better, a payroll tax in real time, eliminates the welfare trap of having your income go down when switching from benefits to a minimum wage, part-time job. According to the Cato Institute, welfare benefits for the average family exceeds the value of working full-time for a minimum wage, for most U.S. states.

Further, the negative income tax transforms the unemployed into an inexpensive workforce for entrepreneurs. This is one example of how society has yet to begin tapping into the power of economic science to improve society.

"the poverty rate was falling until the War on Poverty began."- Cato Institute

"We spend billions of pounds on welfare, yet millions are trapped on welfare. It's not worth their while going into work." - David Cameron

UNION!

There is evidence of trade unions being around as far back as the early middle ages, given that kings went to the trouble of issuing edicts to outlaw them.

They remained illegal in the United Kingdom well into industrialization, including the penalty of execution.

THE HAND THAT WILL RULE THE WORLD - ONE BIG UNION

"When workers combine, masters ... never cease to call aloud for the assistance of the civil magistrate, and the rigorous execution of those laws which have been enacted with so much severity against the combination of servants, labourers, and journeymen." Adam Smith, Wealth of Nations

The first general union was the deceptively named the *Philanthropic Society* in Manchester, U.K., founded in 1818. When unionization laws were relaxed in 1825, British socialists turned their focus to unionization, seeking to increasingly control firms through their unions.

Britain at the time was the most democratic of European countries. The trade unions launched a second front, focusing on expanding suffrage to the workers, relaxing property ownership requirements to run for Parliament, and demanding salaries for Members of Parliament. They were working toward the first Labour Party government with the stated objective of nationalizing key industries. This was achieved when they first achieved a majority government post-WW II.

Eventually, unionization in the U. K. spread to the public sector. There was a series of disruptive strikes of nationalized industries, including nurses, during the 1978/79 "Winter of Discontent". This was the critical point where the uneven socialist playing field *that deferred to workers, to the detriment of consumers*, had played out to its ugly conclusion. Rather than throw off capitalism at that point as predicted by Marx, the citizens got fed up with the reality of advancing socialism and elected Conservative Party Margaret Thatcher, who implemented Chicago School-inspired reforms.

British unions, when granted too much power by voters and government, through inevitable momentum and predictable greed, had moved past the point of optimal social good. In the U.S., the authentically progressive project of worker self-protection, initially against the Gilded Age "Trusts", was implemented by (Republican) Teddy Roosevelt.

FDR's depression-era *Wagner Act,* while containing helpful elements, it resulted in a socialist imbalance against firms with labour increasingly coming under the control of radicals. Union strikes were being used for objectives beyond worker-firm negotiation. This was course-corrected in 1947 by *The Taft-Hartley Act.*

FEEL THE BERN

"Socialist" Senator Bernie Sanders (b. 1941) concluded as a child that politics mattered when he realized that the Holocaust, where many of his relations died, traced back to the democratic election of Hitler.

He ran for political office in high school, took political science at University and was an activist in the 1960s. Sanders became mayor of Burlington, Vermont running as an anti-commercial development candidate, with a margin of 10 votes. He rose to the Senate after serving in the House of Representatives.

He co-founded the Congressional Progressive Caucus, which gathered together the most left-leaning of the Democrats. Sander's rhetoric focusses on criticizing politicians for catering to the rich.

He would like to raise minimum wages but fails to appreciate how this policy hurts the unemployed. He would like to make higher education free by taxing financial transactions but fails to appreciate how this subsidy would in effect skew to the middle and upper middle classes, and drive the financial industry offshore. He wants universal health care but fails to understand the inefficiencies of state management of health care. He would like to roll back right-to-work to encourage trade unions but fails to understand how this drives manufacturing offshore.

He shares with compassionate conservatives concern for the poor, however, "socialists" appear to focus on punishing the rich as their more achievable consolation prize, if not their actual primary objective. None of this is actual socialism, which is state ownership of the means of production, abandoned as a failed experiment, even by the remaining communists, at least the ones not starving. It is rather this endless search for a response to income and wealth inequality, a sincere search for some, but in consortium with rent-seeking, co-dependent political and financial opportunists.

We have on the one hand misguided good intentions with ineffective if not harmful results, and on the other hand, we have a deficiency of sincere compassion toward the economically frustrated, flowing from a deficiency of consciousness, a soft hatred. A co-option of the poor for the socialist's and jealous intellectual's political end of punishing the rich, or selfish and cynical rent-seeking by the statists and labourists.

Sander's quotes:
"we are moving toward an oligarchic form of society, where the billionaires will control the economy and the political life of this country."

"A nation will not survive morally or economically when so few have so much and so many have so little."

CHAPTER 13 - CONSERVATISM

Google defines the word "conservative" as "holding to traditional attitudes and values and cautious about change or innovation, typically in relation to politics or religion." Let's begin by parsing out the many shades of conservatives.

Historically, *Tories* believed in the absolute power of the monarch, a position opposed by the Whigs. *Fiscal* conservatives believe that governments "should live within their means." *Social* conservatives are against abortion and same-sex marriage. *Neo*conservatives are former leftists "who have been mugged by reality".

American *Paleo* or "*classic* conservatives" place particular value on European culture, are isolationist, against multiculturalism and are for limiting immigration. *Liberal* conservatism and conservative *liberalism* support laissez-faire markets and religious tradition, versus *classical* liberalism, which supports freedom of the individual.

Libertarianism overlaps with the laissez-faire aspect of conservatism and the individualism of social liberalism, but has many variants:

- *Right*-libertarians believe in self-reliance to the point of social Darwinism;

- *Constitutionalism* holds law above judiciary;

- *Christian* libertarianism holds that charity and morality should be handled by the Church, without government involvement;

- *Agorism* advocates all relations be voluntary exchanges, with emphasis on employing black markets unauthorized by the state; and,

- *Minarchists* would only retain public policing while *anarcho-capitalists* would go a step further and also privatize the police and the judiciary.

"I am conservative with a small 'c.' It's possible to be conservative in fiscal policy, and tolerant on moral issues or questions of freedom of expression." - Mick Jagger

"There are 100 different doors to come into the conservative movement. You can disagree with 99 of them, as long as you agree on one: more-limited government." - Grover Norquist

EDMUND BURKE, WHIG FATHER OF CONSERVATISM

Burke was an eighteenth-century British writer and Whig reformer politician who was known for opposition to: the American Tea Tax; use of force against the Americans; immoral behaviour of the East India Company; the French revolution; wasteful government spending; and capital punishment.

He was *for* Catholic emancipation; limited constitutional monarchy; limited government; free markets; and free trade.

"We must all obey the great law of change. It is the most powerful law of nature." – Edmund Burke

Nevertheless, though a reformer against royalist Tory intransigence, he is considered to be the father of "Conservatism," which is odd, given that the technical definition of conservatism suggests a preference for the existing order of society or *reactionary* conservatism which seeks to restore the past. The key here is that Burke, against pro-monarch Toryism, was the father of the political ideology of Adam Smith-style, *limited government,* classical liberalism.

"That the State ought to confine itself to what regards the State, or the creatures of the State, ...in a word, to everything that is *truly and properly* public, to the public peace, to the public safety, to the public order, to the public prosperity." – Edmund Burke

The economist Adam Smith remarked that Burke was "the only man I ever knew who thinks on economic subjects exactly as I do, without any previous communications having passed between us."

Burke quotes:

"It is a general popular error to suppose the loudest complainers for the public to be the most anxious for its welfare."

"The only thing necessary for the triumph of evil is for good men to do nothing."

"Nobody made a greater mistake than he who did nothing because he could do only a little."

"Society can overlook murder, adultery or swindling; it never forgives preaching of a new gospel."

AYN RAND, RADICAL FOR CAPITALISM

Alisa Zinov'yevna Rosenbaum (1905-1982)
was born into a prosperous Saint Petersburg
Russian family. They lost everything in the
revolution when she was 12, struggling even to
feed themselves. The silver lining was that
following the revolution, women were
permitted to study at university, and Rand was
one of the first to do so, majoring in history.

She embraced the logic of Aristotle and was
repelled by the mysticism of Plato and Kant.
Following graduation, she studied screen arts,
and assumed the nom de plume "Ayn",
possibly drawn from the Hebrew word ayin, meaning "eye", and Rand, which is a
Cyrillic contraction of Rosenbaum.

She travelled to New York City in 1926 to visit relatives but was so impressed with
the Manhattan skyline she cried "tears of splendor" and determined to stay. She got
her start as a screenwriter for Cecil B. DeMille, where she met her first husband,
Frank O'Connor.

She is known for her best-selling novels *The Fountainhead* (1943) and *Atlas
Shrugged* (1957). *The Fountainhead* criticizes the merit of altruism *taken too far, to
the point of living through others*. Atlas Shrugged makes the point that *it is the
creative industrialists, scientists, and artists who enable a nation's wealth and
economy, and failure to appreciate this, as liberals do, can have grave
consequences.*

Following the financial independence that *The Fountainhead* gave her, she focused
on promoting *Objectivism*, which promoted reason over faith and *ethical* egoism
over altruism. This naturally led to support for economic laissez-faire over
collectivism/statism and support for classical liberalism. She believed libertarianism
was naively close to anarchism. Ultimately, she considered herself a "radical for
capitalism."

Rand and her husband became politically active in the 1940s and acquired a
network of free-market intellectuals, including Austrian School economist, Ludwig
von Mises, who called Rand "the most courageous *man* in America". Having many
admirers in New York, she moved there and conducted informal gatherings with
cult-like elements, which included the attendance of future Federal Reserve
Chairman, Alan Greenspan.

"the concept of man as a heroic being, with his own happiness as the moral purpose
of his life, with productive achievement as his noblest activity, and reason as his
only absolute." Ayn Rand

IRVING KRYSTOL, "GODFATHER OF NEO-CONSERVATISM"

Presidential Medal of Freedom winner Irving Krystol (1920-2009) was a journalist and author, considered to be the Godfather of neoconservatism.

While majoring in history at university, and between graduation and serving in WWII, he was a Trotskyist. With some friends, he published a small magazine, *Enquiry: A Journal of Independent Radical Thought*.

By discharge, he no longer considered himself a socialist, and once famously quipped, *"a neoconservative is a liberal who has been mugged by reality."*

In his book *"Two Cheers for Capitalism"*, which picks up the phrasing of E. M. Forster's *"Two Cheers for Democracy"*, he asserts that capitalism actually works, and secondly, is the most supportive of personal liberty.

However, he acknowledges that capitalism does not provide the existential meaning that socialism provides, leaving neoconservatism, as understood in his time, with a spiritual malaise. Arthur C. Brooks later addressed this challenge.

Socialist Michael Harrington coined the term "neoconservatism" as a pejorative label to describe former liberals such as Krystol, who were inventing a new form of conservatism that respected the limited welfare state of FDR's "New Deal" but rejected "The Great Society" programs of Lyndon Johnson.

Krystol determined the label was apropos and was the first to embrace it. He spent the final decade of his life as a Distinguished Fellow at the American Enterprise Institute.

Irving Kristol Quotes:

"Joining a radical movement when one is young is very much like falling in love when one is young. The girl may turn out to be rotten, but the experience of love is so valuable it can never be entirely undone by the ultimate disenchantment."

"What is wrong with liberalism is liberalism—a metaphysics and a mythology that is woefully blind to human and political reality. . . . It is an ethos that aims simultaneously at political and social collectivism on the one hand, and moral anarchy on the other. It cannot win, but it can make us all losers."

DAVID FRUM - WHY CONSERVATIVES LOSE

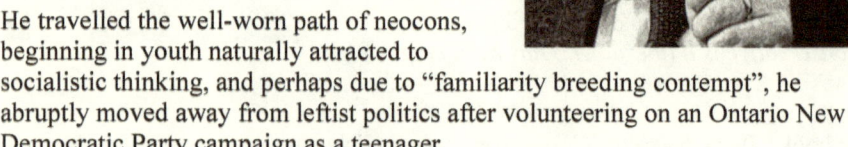

David Frum, son of famous Canadian journalist Barbara Frum, is a neoconservative, Canadian-raised and later naturalized American journalist. He has a Harvard Law degree, undergrad, and an M.A. in history. Part of his significance lies in being a leading Republican intellectual, garnering respect on the right and left, more often seen on MSNBC than Fox News.

He travelled the well-worn path of neocons, beginning in youth naturally attracted to socialistic thinking, and perhaps due to "familiarity breeding contempt", he abruptly moved away from leftist politics after volunteering on an Ontario New Democratic Party campaign as a teenager.

As the old saying most recently popularized by Winston Churchill goes, "anyone who was not a liberal at 20 years of age had no heart, while anyone who was still a liberal at 40 had no head," and Frum, having quite a head, made the transition at an unusually early age.

Following an early journalism career writing for the Wall Street Journal and Forbes magazine, he was to his astonishment recruited to George W. Bush's speechwriting team in the White House, not yet having American citizenship. Following the White House, he worked for the American Enterprise Institute, The National Review, The Daily Beast and The Atlantic.

Unlike other libertarian or neocon writers such as Brooks, who address the political limitations of conservatism by outlining new, softer and more intellectually persuasive communication approaches, Frum more directly attacked supply-siders, Fox News, and evangelicals, marginalizing himself with the Republican Party and conservative media.

His first book, *Dead Right,* in 1994, was a condemnation of most Republican politicians of the early 1990s. His 1996 book, *What's Right,* and his 2000 book, *How We Got Here,* suggests that the 1970s represented an American rebellion against the warrior history, institutions and culture of America.

Following a pair of books on the Iraq war and the presidency of George W. Bush, he returned to the problem of Republican electability in 2008 with *Comeback: Conservatism That Can Win Again.* In 2012 he wrote *Why Romney Lost (and What the GOP Can Do About It),* criticizing out-of-touch economic messaging and out-of-date cultural messaging.

CHAPTER 14 – MARKET PROGRESSIVISM

WHAT ABOUT LIBERTARIANISM?

For reasons mentioned earlier, we should stop referring to capitalism, and rather look for something more helpful. There is libertarianism to consider, but there is a problem with the popular meaning of the word.

Wikipedia defines libertarian as "a political philosophy that upholds liberty as its principal objective. Libertarians seek to maximize autonomy and freedom of choice, emphasizing political freedom, voluntary association and the primacy of individual judgement".

Revolutionary War Gadsden Flag "Don't Tread on Me" Coiled Snake Adopted by Libertarians

How is libertarianism different from neoconservatism, as they both support laissez-faire and are social liberals? The typical libertarian would roll back the size of government to pre-New Deal, removing Food Stamps, Social Security, Medicaid and Medicare, and the Federal Reserve, but would likely keep Teddy Roosevelt's anti-trust and consumer protection regimes.

The word libertarian in popular culture, unfortunately, has come to be associated with an absolutist laissez-faire, not only regarding normal commerce but as well, suggests a sink or swim, survival of the fittest, Ayn Randian Social Darwinism, which the average Westerner sees as objectionable. *The problem with strict libertarianism is that it is inconsistent with human nature.*

Libertarianism is perceived, rightly or wrongly, in the name of personal liberty, to go overboard in opposition to helping those who truly cannot help themselves, in order to avoid the risk of government interference in the life of the average individual.

The Mont Pellerin "classical liberal" economists such as Von Mises, Hayek, and Friedman, reluctantly identified themselves as libertarian, as the word liberal has ironically become associated with Keynesianism, labourism, and statism. However, these economists were not social Darwins, as they support policies such as minimum incomes or the negative income tax.

Though not differing in views, they are not technically neoconservatives, as they did not transition from liberalism to conservatism. Ayn Rand thought libertarianism was too close to anarchism, and rather described herself as a "radical for capitalism."

"I have always found it quaint and rather touching that there is a movement [Libertarians] in the US that thinks Americans are not yet selfish enough."
- Christopher Hitchens

ROTHBARD, FATHER OF MODERN LIBERTARIANISM

Murray Rothbard (1926-1995) began life despising the coerciveness of socialism, stemming from his parents having escaped Russia, openly celebrating America's meritocracy.

Rothbard was apparently one of only two openly Republican students in attendance at Columbia University where he obtained his PhD. Approval of his thesis was delayed by a decade due to his controversial assertion that the government was the underlying cause of the bank panic of 1819.

He later became a student of Von Mises and an expert on his thinking, publishing on Von Mises with the financial support of a philanthropist for a period. Working sometimes part-time on the edge of academia, Rothbard single-handedly launched modern Libertarianism, founding the Center for Libertarian Studies, the Journal of Libertarian Studies, and co-founded the Ludwig von Mises Institute and associated Quarterly Journal of Austrian Economics, as well as the Cato institute.

Rothbard moved beyond the thinking of Von Mises into what he coined, "Anarcho-Capitalism", a branch of Libertarianism and synthesis of Austrian Economics and Individualist Anarchism, the latter which held that all government was a tyranny upon the individual. For example, he advocated policing be provided as a privatized and competitive service.

Rothbard eventually separated from the Libertarian movement and with others developed "Paleolibertarianism", a synthesis between Libertarianism and social or paleo conservativism, a reaction against the libertine and iconoclastic social tendencies of Libertarianism. Presidential candidates Pat Buchannan and Ron Paul would fall in this category.

Rothbard is generally treated as beyond even the fringe of Austrianism due to many controversial views on race and feminism, as well as his record of disparagement of leading figures, including but not limited to Adam Smith, John Maynard Keynes, Milton Friedman and Ayn Rand.

Quotes:
"It is no crime to be ignorant of economics, which is, after all, a specialized discipline and one that most people consider to be a 'dismal science.' But it is totally irresponsible to have a loud and vociferous opinion on economic subjects while remaining in this state of ignorance."

"I frankly don't see anything wrong with greed. I think that the people who are always attacking greed would be more consistent with their position if they refused their next salary increase."

LIBERTARIANISM NEEDS A HEART

Libertarianism then, like the Tinman, needs a heart.

Economic libertarianism, its better half, applied to the interactions of *able* adults, needs to be firewalled from its social policy implications, which leans into social Darwinism toward the economically frustrated.

Let's set aside this social Darwin element. Rather, lets splice it to the original meaning and intent of progressivism, which is *to assertively help the economically frustrated, as an expression of the organic, compassionate nature of humankind.*
Embracing this empathetic intention addresses Krystol's lament regarding the philosophical vulnerability of neoconservatism.

But how is this not inherently oxymoronic? The answer is that **progressivism does not presume blind, no strings income redistribution, in its original meaning!** Rooseveltian, New Deal progressivism, involved public works and jobs for the able and social security for the old, orphaned and disabled, truly focused on assistance for those who could not help themselves, and work for the rest.

The social Darwinism of libertarianism, however, is an impulse that does not arise from our higher nature, as its prime motive is self-sufficiency and independence. It is an ethos of the strong. Progressivism, on the other hand, is an impulse that does arise from our higher nature, at least in principle, but *it is an incomplete, or misdirected intention. It is not yet wedded to empirical pragmaticism, effective non-codependent sustainable assistance, rather than intentions that disregard consequences.*

It is here asserted that free markets of labour, goods, services and, capital, are the most effective default approach to responding to the plight of the *economically frustrated*, ("the poor" who do not wish to be poor). With this, we are defining a new or neo-progressivism, or a Libertarian progressivism which could more descriptively be called "market progressivism."

Market progressivism says what it is, rather than neoprogressivism, which would always need to be explained and would be vulnerable to reinterpretation. Libertarian progressivism is too directly oxymoronic, hence confusing.

"If you analyze it I believe the very heart and soul of conservatism is libertarianism. I think conservatism is really a misnomer just as liberalism is a misnomer for the liberals — if we were back in the days of the Revolution, so-called conservatives today would be the Liberals and the liberals would be the Tories. The basis of conservatism is a desire for less government interference or less centralized authority or more individual freedom and this is a pretty general description also of what libertarianism is." - Ronald Reagan

FRANK S. MEYER'S FUSIONISM

When Meyer was at the London School of Economics in the 1930s he became the student union president but was deported back to America for communist activism. Serving during the war, he converted to classical liberalism after reading F.A. Hayek's *The Road to Serfdom*.

As Associate Editor for National Review magazine in the 1950s, Meyer's writings attempted to "fuse" libertarianism and social conservatism as "modern conservatism."

His core assertion is that *libertarian freedom is dependent on authentic virtue which co-evolves with tradition, including religious tradition, philosophy, or humanism*, rather than the artificially imposed virtue of state income redistribution or social planning.

In his book *In Defense of Freedom*, he asserts that beyond its essential purpose of limiting coercion between individuals, the state inevitably becomes an agent of coercion itself, not to mention the corruptions of institutional moral hazard, when it sets out to impose virtuous behaviour on citizens.

Meyer's Fusionism Asserts Libertarianism requires a Moral Citizenry Arising From Natural Causes such as Religious Tradition, Philosophy or Humanism

Hence, small and decentralized government is not only about financial sustainability but is as well an objective that flows from the need to express the natural virtue of citizens arising from a co-evolving tradition, in the context of liberty, free from government direction and limitation.

Modern fusionists argue that George Bush's expansion of government, motivated by compassionate conservatism, in particular, the prescription drug program, as well as the great recession stimulus, was a betrayal of the principle of small government.

"It's especially hard to believe that it was only a decade ago, on a cold April day on a small hill in upstate New York, that another of these great thinkers, Frank Meyer, was buried. He'd made the awful journey that so many others had: he pulled himself from the clutches of 'The [communist] God That Failed,' and then in his writing fashioned a vigorous new synthesis of traditional and libertarian thought – a synthesis that is today recognized by many as modern conservatism." Ronald Reagan

COMPASSIONATE, BLEEDING HEART CONSERVATISM

The power of free markets to liberate the poor is somewhat confusingly described as Conservatism. When the intention is clarified as compassion, we arrive at George Bush's "compassionate" conservatism. This term was first coined by U.S. Historian Doug Weed, who in 1979 gave a speech entitled *"The Compassionate Conservative."*

He argued that for many the motivation behind Republican conservatism wasn't to conserve anything, nor defend personal liberty. Rather, it was compassion, asserting that the sometimes revolutionary restorative intent of the free marketplace is what serves the economically frustrated best. He also described this view as "bleeding heart conservatism".

Bush Adopts Compassionate Conservatism

George W. Bush hired Weed as an aide and picked up the term from him. It was a key slogan in his 2000 presidential campaign. Dr. Marvin Olasky memorialized the term in his 1996 book *Renewing American Compassion* and his 2000 book *Compassionate Conservatism: What it is, What it Does, and how it Can Transform America*. Bush wrote the foreword to the latter book, and Olasky is considered to be the "godfather of compassionate conservatism."

"It's great that we got a compassionate conservative, but to me, that sounds like a Volvo with a gun rack" - Robin Williams

So again, compassionate conservatism is not really about conservation or the status quo. It is rather about a revolution of the restoration of liberty, libertarianism in economic affairs. This turns out as well to be the most effective and caring social policy for the able and prudent, if constrained by common sense.

While bleeding heart conservatism contains the meaning of market progressivism, as it is more broadly about free markets than conservatism, the nomenclature is misleading, inaccurate, non-descriptive, and unhelpful.

"Compassionate conservatives [...] offer a new way of thinking about the poor. They know that telling the poor that they are mere passive victims, whether of racism or of vast economic forces, is not only false but also destructive, paralyzing the poor with thoughts of their own helplessness and inadequacy. The poor need the larger society's moral support; they need to hear the message of personal responsibility and self-reliance, the optimistic assurance that if they try – as they must – they will make it. They need to know, too, that they can't blame "the system" for their own wrongdoing." - Myron Magnet

"PROGRESSIVE," THE WORD

Progressive is such a positive word, it was adopted by a company for its brand name! Who could not like and endorse anything that is "progressive"?

Google defines the word two ways, let's look at the first definition, "happening or developing gradually or in stages; proceeding step by step."

This suggests a certain step by step inevitability to progressivism, and implies that anyone who is not "progressive," is on the wrong side of history, is against progress, and must therefore by implication, be "regressive."

The Fictional Flo of
Progressive Insurance

Now, regressive cannot be a good thing, can it? Regressive gene comes to mind, or regressive tax. Sounds pretty awful. There are no companies named "Regressive". So, simply the nominal sound of the word progressive gives it an unfair advantage. So why do opponents of political progressivism use the moniker to label the opposition?

The other meaning of progressive is "a person advocating or implementing social reform or new, liberal ideas". So, taken together, progressives are "progressing with progressivism", step by step, implementing, a) social reform b) new ideas and/or c) liberal ideas.

There is an implication in all this that social reform must be a good thing, ... right? Who of good intention could be against social reform, or the core intention of political progressivism, which is to help the poor, as a significant part of the progressive project of moving from barbarism to civilization?

Good people are motivated by empathy, insecure people are motivated by guilt, even a sociopath can be irritated or threatened by the aesthetic deficiencies, problems and personal risks related to surrounding poverty.

So, not helping the poor, let alone exploiting the poor, is a minority view, perhaps held by rednecks, racists, and some extremist libertarians. Not nice people. On the face of things, being a progressive who cares about the poor, seems to be the correct way to be, if you are thoughtful, sensitive person. Right? Are you starting to see the problem here?

Market-oriented thinkers need to rethink and "focus group" on the words they use to publicize their world view.

THE FREE MARKET PROGRESSIVE MANIFESTO

1) Unlike libertarianism, which focuses on protecting the strong from government, the fundamental driver of *market* progressivism is the intention to elevate the economically frustrated in society.

2) Unlike Robin Hood progressivism, market progressivism follows the empirical evidence of economic science, wherever that leads.

3) Unlike the apparently oxymoronic "compassionate conservatism", market progressivism is a more accurate and marketable moniker for market-based, measurably effective compassion.

4) Unlike "We are the 99%" movement progressivism, market progressivism measures absolute rather than relative performance in elevating the economically frustrated, consequently, is agnostic on so-called income disparity.

5) Unlike Robin Hood communism, socialism, liberalism and progressivism, market progressivism holds that work, thrift, savings, investment, capital, and entrepreneurship are the engines of job creation and higher wages, therefore should be encouraged by tax and social policy.

6) So-called "progressive" taxation should be dialed back from these beneficial activities and rather be replaced with highly progressive consumption, emmigration exit, luxury and other taxes that are job and productivity neutral.

7) Minimum wages, unemployment insurance, welfare, food stamps, and public housing, should be replaced with generous training, workfare and a wage top-up (negative payroll/income tax) that eliminates disincentive traps.

8) Government should wage war on unemployment and other authentic market failures, but itself be otherwise minimized and privatized where practical, because:

   a) Government deficit-spending is intergenerational theft, and hence, immoral.

   b) Taxes are a disincentive to the drivers of job creation and workers' wages on the one hand, and grow wasteful government on the other hand.

   c) Government activity is inherently prone to wastefulness due to: the lack of discipline of competition; the lack of profit measurement; the lack of external regulation; and, due to the existence of perverse incentives to expand bureaucracies and not solve problems.

"The world is a dangerous place to live not because of the people who are evil, but because of the people who don't do anything about it." Albert Einstein

"The difficulty lies not so much in developing new ideas as in escaping from old ones." John Maynard Keynes

"Let us overthrow the totems, break the taboos, or better, let us consider them cancelled. Coldly, let us be intelligent." Pierre Trudeau

Author Contact
randy.kroeker@gmail.com

www.ingramcontent.com/pod-product-compliance
Lightning Source LLC
Chambersburg PA
CBHW022108170526
45157CB00004B/1537